MSA · eBBR 2017
Original-Prüfungsaufgaben mit Lösungen

Englisch

Berlin · Brandenburg

2012–2016

MP3-CD

STARK

© 2016 Stark Verlag GmbH
7. ergänzte Auflage
www.stark-verlag.de

Das Werk und alle seine Bestandteile sind urheberrechtlich geschützt. Jede vollständige oder teilweise Vervielfältigung, Verbreitung und Veröffentlichung bedarf der ausdrücklichen Genehmigung des Verlages.

Inhalt

Vorwort
Hinweise zur Abschlussprüfung

Kurzgrammatik

Besonderheiten einiger Wortarten .... G 1
1 Adjektive und Adverbien – *Adjectives and Adverbs* .... G 1
2 Artikel – *Article* .... G 5
3 Pronomen – *Pronouns* .... G 6
4 Präpositionen – *Prepositions* .... G 8
5 Modale Hilfsverben – *Modal Auxiliaries* .... G 9

Infinitiv, Gerundium oder Partizip? – Die infiniten Verbformen   G 10
6 Infinitiv – *Infinitive* .... G 10
7 Gerundium (*-ing*-Form) – *Gerund* .... G 11
8 Infinitiv oder Gerundium? – *Infinitive or Gerund?* .... G 13
9 Partizipien – *Participles* .... G 14

Bildung und Gebrauch der finiten Verbformen .... G 17
10 Zeiten – *Tenses* .... G 17
11 Passiv – *Passive Voice* .... G 24

Der Satz im Englischen .... G 25
12 Wortstellung – *Word Order* .... G 25
13 Konditionalsätze – *Conditional Sentences* .... G 25
14 Relativsätze – *Relative Clauses* .... G 27
15 Indirekte Rede – *Reported Speech* .... G 29

Anhang .... G 31
16 Liste wichtiger unregelmäßiger Verben –
   List of Irregular Verbs .... G 31

Original-Prüfungsaufgaben

MSA 2012
- Listening 2012-1
- Reading 2012-6
- Writing 2012-16
- Lösungsvorschläge 2012-20

MSA 2013
- Listening 2013-1
- Reading 2013-7
- Writing 2013-18
- Lösungsvorschläge 2013-22

MSA und eBBR 2014
- Listening 2014-1
- Reading 2014-8
- Writing 2014-19
- Lösungsvorschläge 2014-23

MSA und eBBR 2015
- Listening 2015-1
- Reading 2015-8
- Writing 2015-20
- Lösungsvorschläge 2015-24

MSA und eBBR 2016
- Listening 2016-1
- Reading 2016-8
- Writing 2016-20
- Lösungsvorschläge 2016-24

MP3-CD

MSA 2012
Listening Part 1: Conversations	Track 1
Listening Part 2: Radio Ads	Track 2
Listening Part 3: Ellis Island	Track 3
Listening Part 4: CouchSurfing	Track 4

MSA 2013
Listening Part 1: Voicemail Messages	Track 5
Listening Part 2: Radio Ads	Track 6
Listening Part 3: The Globe Theatre	Track 7
Listening Part 4: Extreme Sports	Track 8

MSA und eBBR 2014
Listening Part 1: Recorded Messages	Track 9
Listening Part 2: Radio Ads	Track 10
Listening Part 3: Unusual Hobbies	Track 11
Listening Part 4: Dumpster Diving	Track 12

MSA und eBBR 2015
Listening Part 1: Short Messages	Track 13
Listening Part 2: Radio Ads	Track 14
Listening Part 3: World Alternative Games	Track 15
Listening Part 4: Fast Fashion	Track 16

MSA und eBBR 2016
Listening Part 1: Short Messages	Track 17
Listening Part 2: Radio Ads	Track 18
Listening Part 3: Schools Around the World	Track 19
Listening Part 4: Hotel Mom and Dad	Track 20

Die Hintergrundgeräusche auf der MP3-CD stammen aus folgenden Quellen: Freesound, Pacdv, Partners in Rhyme und Soundsnap.

Jeweils zu Beginn des neuen Schuljahres erscheinen die neuen Ausgaben der Abschlussprüfungsaufgaben mit Lösungen.

Vorwort

Liebe Schülerin, lieber Schüler,

dieses Buch enthält die **Original-Prüfungen 2012 bis 2016** zur intensiven Vorbereitung auf den **Mittleren Schulabschluss** und die **erweiterte Berufsbildungsreife** im Fach **Englisch 2017**. Es ist insbesondere für die **Vorbereitungsphase unmittelbar vor der Prüfung** gedacht und hilft dir dabei, noch mehr Sicherheit im Umgang mit Prüfungsaufgaben zu gewinnen. Mithilfe der **Original-Prüfungsaufgaben und Lösungsvorschläge** kannst du testen, ob du für den „Ernstfall" gut gerüstet bist. Versuche, den Hörverstehenstest in 45 Minuten, den Test zum Leseverstehen und Schreiben in 105 Minuten zu bearbeiten – diese Zeit steht dir auch in der Prüfung zur Verfügung. Kontrolliere erst danach deine Lösungen. Hast du viele Fehler gemacht bzw. hat dir die vorgegebene Zeit nicht ausgereicht, arbeite die Aufgaben noch einmal durch. Wenn du nur sehr wenige oder gar keine Fehler gemacht hast, kannst du ganz entspannt in die Prüfung gehen.

Die beiliegende **MP3-CD** enthält alle Hörverstehenstexte der Original-Prüfungen. Sie hilft dir dabei, dein Hörverständnis gezielt zu verbessern.

In der **Kurzgrammatik** werden alle wichtigen grammatischen Themen knapp erläutert und an Beispielsätzen veranschaulicht. Hier kannst du nachschlagen, wenn du in der Grammatik einmal unsicher sein solltest.

Der Band „**Training 2017: MSA und eBBR**" (Best.-Nr. 111550) bietet dir weiterführende Übungsmöglichkeiten. Er enthält neben der Original-Prüfung 2016 zahlreiche Übungsaufgaben zu allen prüfungsrelevanten Kompetenzbereichen. Darüber hinaus werden dir Strategien zur effektiven Bearbeitung der Aufgaben vermittelt. So kannst du deine sprachlichen Fertigkeiten gezielt trainieren und dich langfristig auf die Prüfung vorbereiten.

Sollten nach Erscheinen dieses Bandes noch wichtige Änderungen in der Prüfung 2017 vom LISUM Berlin-Brandenburg bekannt gegeben werden, findest du aktuelle Informationen dazu im Internet unter:
www.stark-verlag.de/pruefung-aktuell

Viel Spaß beim Üben und viel Erfolg in der Prüfung!

Autoren:

Lösungen Prüfungsaufgaben: Frank Lemke, Kathryn Nussdorf

Hinweise zur Abschlussprüfung

In Berlin und Brandenburg müssen sich alle Schülerinnen und Schüler der 10. Klasse einer Prüfung unterziehen. Seit dem Schuljahr 2013/14 kann im Fach Englisch mit derselben Prüfung die erweiterte Berufsbildungsreife (eBBR) erlangt werden. Für den Erwerb der eBBR musst du grundlegende Aufgaben lösen, für den MSA zusätzlich noch anspruchsvollere Aufgaben, die durch ein Sternchen (✶) gekennzeichnet sind. Es ist für die Abschlüsse jedoch nicht von Bedeutung, in welchen der Aufgaben durch eine korrekte Bearbeitung die Punkte erzielt werden. Alle Aufgaben zählen genauso für den MSA wie für die eBBR.

Der MSA wird in einem Abschlussverfahren erworben, das sich wie folgt zusammensetzt:
- Jahrgangsnoten der 10. Klasse
- zentrale schriftliche Prüfungen in den Fächern Deutsch, Mathematik und der ersten Fremdsprache
- mündliche Prüfung in der ersten Fremdsprache
- Präsentationsprüfung in einem gesellschaftswissenschaftlichen, naturwissenschaftlichen, künstlerischen oder Wahlpflichtfach

Bei den Prüfungen zum mittleren Schulabschluss und zur erweiterten Berufsbildungsreife geht es nicht nur um erlerntes Wissen, sondern in erster Linie um **Kompetenzen** oder Fertigkeiten, die in der Sekundarstufe I erworben wurden. Im Fach Englisch wird bei diesen Fertigkeiten zwischen den Bereichen Hörverständnis, Leseverständnis, Schreiben und Sprechen unterschieden. Folglich werden weder Vokabeln noch theoretisches Grammatikwissen abgefragt, sondern es wird geprüft, ...
- ob du den Inhalt eines von Muttersprachlern gesprochenen Textes trotz einiger unbekannter Wörter erfassen kannst („**Listening**"),
- ob du einen unbekannten Text durch stilles Lesen verstehst („**Reading**"),
- ob du Formulare ausfüllen, auf Nachrichten in einem Online-Forum reagieren und die Kernaussagen deutscher Texte auf Englisch wiedergeben kannst („**Writing**"),
- ob du in der Lage bist, auf Englisch ein Gespräch zu führen, auf Fragen angemessen zu reagieren, Vorschläge zu machen und zu diskutieren („**Speaking**").

Schriftliche Prüfung
Die schriftliche Prüfung besteht aus den Teilen Hörverstehen, Leseverstehen und Schreiben. Sie beginnt mit dem Hörverständnisteil. Die Bearbeitungszeit ist von der Länge der Texte auf der CD abhängig. Dieser Prüfungsteil dauert ca. 45 Minuten. Erst nach dem Ende der Hörtexte werden die Lösungen auf das „**Answer Sheet**" übertragen.
Im Anschluss stehen für die Aufgaben zum Leseverstehen und Schreiben ca. 105 Minuten zur Verfügung. Auch beim Leseverstehen musst du deine Antworten in ein „**Answer Sheet**" übertragen.

Mündliche Prüfung
Die Sprechfertigkeit wird zu einem anderen Termin geprüft. Es handelt sich hierbei um eine Partnerprüfung von maximal 15 Minuten.

Kurzgrammatik

Besonderheiten einiger Wortarten

1 Adjektive und Adverbien – *Adjectives and Adverbs*
Bildung und Verwendung von Adverbien – *Formation and Use of Adverbs*

Bildung		
Adjektiv + *-ly*	glad	→ gladly
Ausnahmen:		
• *-y* am Wortende wird zu *-i*	easy	→ easily
	funny	→ funnily
• auf einen Konsonanten folgendes *-le* wird zu *-ly*	simple	→ simply
	probable	→ probably
• *-ic* am Wortende wird zu *-ically*	fantastic	→ fantastically
Ausnahme:	public	→ publicly

Beachte:
- Unregelmäßig gebildet wird: good → well
- Endet das Adjektiv auf *-ly*, so kann kein Adverb gebildet werden; man verwendet deshalb:
  in a + Adjektiv + *manner/way*   friendly → in a friendly manner
- In einigen Fällen haben Adjektiv und Adverb dieselbe Form, z. B.: daily, early, fast, hard, long, low, weekly, yearly
- Manche Adjektive bilden zwei Adverbformen, die sich in der Bedeutung unterscheiden, z. B.:

Adj./Adv.	Adv. auf *-ly*
hard	hardly
schwierig, hart	kaum
late	lately
spät	neulich, kürzlich
near	nearly
nahe	beinahe

The task is hard.   (adjective)
Die Aufgabe ist schwierig.
She works hard.   (adverb)
Sie arbeitet hart.
She hardly works.   (adverb)
Sie arbeitet kaum.

Verwendung
Adverbien bestimmen
- Verben,

- Adjektive,

- andere Adverbien oder

- einen ganzen Satz näher.

She <u>easily</u> <u>found</u> her brother in the crowd.
Sie fand ihren Bruder leicht in der Menge.
This band is <u>extremely</u> <u>famous</u>.
Diese Band ist sehr berühmt.
He walks <u>extremely</u> <u>quickly</u>.
Er geht äußerst schnell.
<u>Fortunately</u>, <u>nobody was hurt</u>.
Glücklicherweise wurde niemand verletzt.

Beachte:
Nach bestimmten Verben steht nicht das Adverb, sondern das Adjektiv:
- Verben, die einen **Zustand** ausdrücken, z. B.:

to be	sein
to become	werden
to get	werden
to seem	scheinen
to stay	bleiben

- Verben der **Sinneswahrnehmung**, z. B.:

to feel	sich anfühlen
to look	aussehen
to smell	riechen
to sound	sich anhören
to taste	schmecken

Everything <u>seems</u> <u>quiet</u>.
Alles scheint ruhig zu sein.

This dress <u>looks</u> <u>fantastic</u>!
Dieses Kleid sieht toll aus!

Steigerung des Adjektivs – *Comparison of Adjectives*

Bildung
Man unterscheidet:
- Grundform/Positiv *(positive)*
- Komparativ *(comparative)*
- Superlativ *(superlative)*

Peter is <u>young</u>.
Jane is <u>younger</u>.
Paul is <u>the youngest</u>.

Steigerung auf -er, -est
- einsilbige Adjektive

- zweisilbige Adjektive, die auf
  -er, -le, -ow oder -y enden

old, old<u>er</u>, old<u>est</u>
alt, älter, am ältesten

clever, clever<u>er</u>, clever<u>est</u>
klug, klüger, am klügsten

simp<u>le</u>, simp<u>ler</u>, simp<u>lest</u>
einfach, einfacher, am einfachsten

narrow, narrow<u>er</u>, narrow<u>est</u>
eng, enger, am engsten

funny, funn<u>ier</u>, funn<u>iest</u>
lustig, lustiger, am lustigsten

Beachte:
- stummes -e am Wortende entfällt
- nach einem Konsonanten wird
  -y am Wortende zu -i-
- nach kurzem Vokal wird ein Konsonant am Wortende verdoppelt

simp<u>le</u>, simp<u>ler</u>, simp<u>lest</u>

funn<u>y</u>, funn<u>ier</u>, funn<u>iest</u>

fi<u>t</u>, fi<u>tt</u>er, fi<u>tt</u>est

Steigerung mit *more ..., most ...*
- zweisilbige Adjektive, die nicht
  auf -er, -le, -ow oder -y enden
- Adjektive mit drei und mehr
  Silben

useful, <u>more</u> useful, <u>most</u> useful
nützlich, nützlicher, am nützlichsten

difficult, <u>more</u> difficult, <u>most</u> difficult
schwierig, schwieriger, am schwierigsten

Unregelmäßige Steigerung
Die unregelmäßig gesteigerten
Adjektive muss man auswendig
lernen. Einige sind hier angegeben:

good, better, best
gut, besser, am besten

bad, worse, worst
schlecht, schlechter, am schlechtesten

many, more, most
viele, mehr, am meisten

much, more, most
viel, mehr, am meisten

little, less, least
wenig, weniger, am wenigsten

Steigerungsformen im Satz – *Sentences with Comparisons*

Es gibt folgende Möglichkeiten, Steigerungen im Satz zu verwenden:
- **Positiv:** Zwei oder mehr Personen oder Sachen sind **gleich oder ungleich:** *(not) as* + Grundform des Adjektivs + *as*

  Anne is <u>as</u> tall <u>as</u> John (and Steve).
  Anne ist genauso groß wie John (und Steve).
  John is <u>not as</u> tall <u>as</u> Steve.
  John ist nicht so groß wie Steve.

- **Komparativ:** Zwei oder mehr Personen/Sachen sind **verschieden** (größer/besser …): Komparativform des Adjektivs + *than*

  Steve is tall<u>er</u> <u>than</u> Anne.
  Steve ist größer als Anne.

- **Superlativ:** Eine Person oder Sache wird besonders hervorgehoben (der/die/das größte/beste …): *the* + Superlativform des Adjektivs

  Steve is <u>the</u> tall<u>est</u> boy in class.
  Steve ist der größte Junge in der Klasse.

Steigerung des Adverbs – *Comparison of Adverbs*

Adverbien können wie Adjektive auch gesteigert werden.
- Adverbien auf *-ly* werden mit *more, most* bzw. mit *less, least* gesteigert.

  She talks <u>more</u> <u>quickly</u> than John.
  Sie spricht schneller als John.

- Adverbien, die dieselbe Form wie das Adjektiv haben, werden mit *-er, -est* gesteigert.

  fast   – fast<u>er</u> – fast<u>est</u>
  early   – earl<u>ier</u> – earl<u>iest</u>

- Manche Adverbien haben unregelmäßige Steigerungsformen, z. B.:

  well   – better – best
  badly – worse – worst
  little – less   – least
  much   – more   – most

Die Stellung von Adverbien im Satz

Adverbien können verschiedene Positionen im Satz einnehmen:
- Am **Anfang des Satzes**, vor dem Subjekt *(front position)*

  <u>Tomorrow</u> he will be in London.
  Morgen [betont] wird er in London sein.
  <u>Unfortunately</u>, I can't come to the party.
  Leider kann ich nicht zur Party kommen.

- **Im Satz** *(mid position)*
  vor dem Vollverb,

  nach *to be*,

  nach dem ersten Hilfsverb.

- **Am Ende des Satzes** *(end position)*

  Gibt es mehrere Adverbien am Satzende, so gilt die **Reihenfolge**: Art und Weise – Ort – Zeit *(manner – place – time)*

She <u>often</u> goes to school by bike.
Sie fährt oft mit dem Rad in die Schule.
She is <u>already</u> at home.
Sie ist schon zu Hause.
You can <u>even</u> go swimming there.
Man kann dort sogar schwimmen gehen.
He will be in London <u>tomorrow</u>.
Er wird morgen in London sein.

The snow melts <u>slowly</u> <u>in the mountains</u> at <u>springtime</u>.
Im Frühling schmilzt der Schnee langsam in den Bergen.

2 Artikel – *Article*

Der **bestimmte Artikel** steht, wenn man von einer **ganz bestimmten Person oder Sache** spricht.

<u>The</u> cat is sleeping on the sofa.
Die Katze schläft auf dem Sofa. [nicht irgendeine Katze, sondern eine bestimmte]

Beachte: Der bestimmte Artikel steht unter anderem **immer** in folgenden Fällen:
- **abstrakte Begriffe**, die näher erläutert sind
- **Gebäudebezeichnungen**, wenn man vom Gebäude und nicht von der Institution spricht
- **Eigennamen im Plural** (Familiennamen, Gebirge, Inselgruppen, einige Länder etc.)
- Namen von **Flüssen** und **Meeren**

<u>The</u> agriculture practised in the USA is very successful.
Die Landwirtschaft, wie sie in den USA praktiziert wird, ist sehr erfolgreich.

<u>The</u> university should be renovated soon.
Die Universität sollte bald renoviert werden.

<u>the</u> Johnsons, <u>the</u> Rockies, <u>the</u> Hebrides, <u>the</u> Netherlands, <u>the</u> USA

<u>the</u> Mississippi, <u>the</u> North Sea, <u>the</u> Pacific Ocean

Der **unbestimmte Artikel** steht, wenn man von einer **nicht näher bestimmten Person oder Sache** spricht.

<u>A</u> man is walking down the road.
Ein Mann läuft gerade die Straße entlang. [irgendein Mann]

Beachte:
In einigen Fällen steht **stets** der unbestimmte Artikel:
- **Berufsbezeichnungen** und **Nationalitäten**

  She is an engineer. *Sie ist Ingenieurin.*
  He is a Scot(sman). *Er ist Schotte.*

- Zugehörigkeit zu einer **Religion** oder **Partei**

  She is a Catholic. *Sie ist katholisch.*
  He is a Tory. *Er ist Mitglied der Tories.*

In diesen Fällen steht **kein Artikel**:
- **nicht zählbare** Nomen wie z. B. **Stoffbezeichnungen**

  Gold is very valuable.
  Gold ist sehr wertvoll.

- **abstrakte Nomen** ohne nähere Bestimmung

  Buddhism is widespread in Asia.
  Der Buddhismus ist in Asien weit verbreitet.

- **Kollektivbegriffe**, z. B. *man, youth, society*

  Man is responsible for global warming.
  Der Mensch ist für die Klimaerwärmung verantwortlich.

- **Institutionen**, z. B. *school, church, university, prison*

  We went to school together.
  Wir gingen zusammen zur Schule.

- **Mahlzeiten**, z. B. *breakfast, lunch*

  Dinner is at 8 p.m.
  Das Abendessen ist um 20 Uhr.

- *by* + **Verkehrsmittel**

  I went to school by bike.
  Ich fuhr mit dem Fahrrad zur Schule.

- **Personennamen** (auch mit Titel), **Verwandtschaftsbezeichnungen**, die wie Namen verwendet werden

  Tom, Mr Scott, Queen Elizabeth, Dr Hill, Dad, Uncle Harry

- Bezeichnungen für **Straßen, Plätze, Brücken, Parkanlagen**

  Fifth Avenue, Trafalgar Square, Westminster Bridge, Hyde Park

- Namen von **Ländern, Kontinenten, Städten, Seen, Inseln, Bergen**

  France, Asia, San Francisco, Loch Ness, Corsica, Ben Nevis

3 Pronomen – *Pronouns*

Possessivpronomen – *Possessive Pronouns*

Possessivpronomen (*possessive pronouns*) verwendet man, um zu sagen, **wem etwas gehört**.
Steht ein Possessivpronomen allein, so wird eine andere Form verwendet als in Verbindung mit einem Substantiv:

mit Substantiv	ohne Substantiv			
my	mine	This is my bike.	–	This is mine.
your	yours	This is your bike.	–	This is yours.
his/her/its	his/hers/–	This is her bike.	–	This is hers.
our	ours	This is our bike.	–	This is ours.
your	yours	This is your bike.	–	This is yours.
their	theirs	This is their bike.	–	This is theirs.

Reflexivpronomen – *Reflexive Pronouns*

Reflexivpronomen *(reflexive pronouns)* **beziehen sich auf das Subjekt** des Satzes **zurück**. Es handelt sich also um dieselbe Person:

myself	I will buy myself a new car.
yourself	You will buy yourself a new car.
himself / herself / itself	He will buy himself a new car.
ourselves	We will buy ourselves a new car.
yourselves	You will buy yourselves a new car.
themselves	They will buy themselves a new car.

Beachte:
- Einige Verben stehen ohne Reflexivpronomen, obwohl im Deutschen mit „mich, dich, sich etc." übersetzt wird.

  I apologize …
  Ich entschuldige mich …
  He is hiding.
  Er versteckt sich.

- Einige Verben können sowohl mit einem Objekt als auch mit einem Reflexivpronomen verwendet werden. Dabei ändert sich die Bedeutung, z. B. bei *to control, to enjoy, to help, to occupy.*

  He is enjoying the party.
  Er genießt die Party.
  She is enjoying herself.
  Sie amüsiert sich.
  He is helping the child.
  Er hilft dem Kind.
  Help yourself!
  Bedienen Sie sich!

Reziprokes Pronomen – *Reciprocal Pronoun* ("each other / one another")

each other / one another ist unveränderlich. Es bezieht sich auf **zwei oder mehr Personen** und wird mit „sich (gegenseitig)/einander" übersetzt.	They looked at each other and laughed. *Sie schauten sich (gegenseitig) an und lachten.* *oder:* *Sie schauten einander an und lachten.*
Beachte: Einige Verben stehen ohne *each other*, obwohl im Deutschen mit „sich" übersetzt wird.	to meet — *sich treffen* to kiss — *sich küssen* to fall in love — *sich verlieben*

4 Präpositionen – *Prepositions*

Präpositionen *(prepositions)* drücken **räumliche, zeitliche oder andere Arten von Beziehungen** aus.

The ball is under the table.
He came home after six o'clock.

Die wichtigsten Präpositionen mit Beispielen für ihre Verwendung:

- *at*
  Ortsangabe: *at home* — I'm at home now. *Ich bin jetzt zu Hause.*
  Zeitangabe: *at 3 p.m.* — He arrived at 3 p.m. *Er kam um 15 Uhr an.*

- *by*
  Angabe des Mittels: *by bike* — She went to work by bike. *Sie fuhr mit dem Rad zur Arbeit.*

  Angabe der Ursache: *by mistake* — He did it by mistake. *Er hat es aus Versehen getan.*

  Zeitangabe: *by tomorrow* — You will get the letter by tomorrow. *Du bekommst den Brief bis morgen.*

- *for*
  Zeitdauer: *for hours* — We waited for the bus for hours. *Wir warteten stundenlang auf den Bus.*

- *from*
  Ortsangabe: *from Dublin* — Ian is from Dublin. *Ian kommt aus Dublin.*

  Zeitangabe: *from nine to five* — We work from nine to five. *Wir arbeiten von neun bis fünf Uhr.*

- *in*
  Ortsangabe: *in England* — In England, they drive on the left. *In England herrscht Linksverkehr.*

Zeitangabe: *in the morning*

- *of*
  Ortsangabe: *north of the city*

- *on*
  Ortsangabe: *on the left,*
  on the floor
  Zeitangabe: *on Monday*

- *to*
  Richtungsangabe: *to the left*

  Angabe des Ziels: *to London*

They woke up <u>in the morning</u>.
Sie wachten am Morgen auf.

The village lies <u>north of the city</u>.
Das Dorf liegt nördlich der Stadt.

<u>On the left</u> you see the London Eye.
Links sehen Sie das London Eye.

<u>On Monday</u> she will buy the tickets.
(Am) Montag kauft sie die Karten.

Please turn <u>to the left</u>.
Bitte wenden Sie sich nach links.

He goes <u>to London</u> every year.
Er fährt jedes Jahr nach London.

5 Modale Hilfsverben – *Modal Auxiliaries*

Zu den **modalen Hilfsverben** *(modal auxiliaries)* zählen z. B. *can, may* und *must*.

Bildung

- Die modalen Hilfsverben haben für alle Personen **nur eine Form**: kein -*s* in der 3. Person Singular.

  I, you, he/she/it,
  we, you, they } must

- Auf ein modales Hilfsverb folgt der **Infinitiv ohne** *to*.

  You <u>must</u> <u>listen</u> to my new CD.
  Du musst dir meine neue CD anhören.

- **Frage und Verneinung** werden nicht mit *do/did* umschrieben.

  <u>Can</u> you help me, please?
  Kannst du mir bitte helfen?

Die modalen Hilfsverben können nicht alle Zeiten bilden. Deshalb benötigt man **Ersatzformen** (können auch im Präsens verwendet werden).

- *can* (können)
  Ersatzformen:
  (to) be able to (Fähigkeit),
  (to) be allowed to (Erlaubnis)

  I <u>can</u> sing. / I <u>was able to</u> sing.
  Ich kann singen. / Ich konnte singen.
  You <u>can't</u> go to the party. /
  I <u>wasn't allowed to</u> go to the party.
  Du darfst nicht auf die Party gehen. /
  Ich durfte nicht auf die Party gehen.

  Beachte: Im *simple past* und *conditional I* ist auch *could* möglich.

  When I was three, I <u>could</u> already ski.
  Mit drei konnte ich schon Ski fahren.

- **may** (dürfen) – sehr höflich
  Ersatzform: *(to) be allowed to*

  You <u>may</u> go home early. /
  You <u>were allowed to</u> go home early.
  Du darfst früh nach Hause gehen. /
  Du durftest früh nach Hause gehen.

- **must** (müssen)
  Ersatzform: *(to) have to*

  He <u>must</u> be home by ten o'clock. /
  He <u>had to</u> be home by ten o'clock.
  Er muss um zehn Uhr zu Hause sein. /
  Er musste um zehn Uhr zu Hause sein.

Beachte:
must not/mustn't = „nicht dürfen"

You <u>must not</u> eat all the cake.
Du darfst nicht den ganzen Kuchen essen.

„nicht müssen, nicht brauchen" =
not have to, needn't

You <u>don't have to</u>/<u>needn't</u> eat all the cake.
Du musst nicht den ganzen Kuchen essen. /
Du brauchst nicht ... zu essen.

Infinitiv, Gerundium oder Partizip? – Die infiniten Verbformen

6 Infinitiv – *Infinitive*

Der **Infinitiv** (Grundform des Verbs) mit *to* steht z. B. nach
- bestimmten **Verben**, z. B.:

to decide	(sich) entscheiden, beschließen
to expect	erwarten
to hope	hoffen
to manage	schaffen
to plan	planen
to promise	versprechen
to want	wollen

He <u>decided</u> <u>to wait</u>.
Er beschloss zu warten.

- bestimmten **Substantiven und Pronomen** *(something, anything)*, z. B.:

attempt	Versuch
idea	Idee
plan	Plan
wish	Wunsch

We haven't got <u>anything</u> <u>to eat</u> at home.
Wir haben nichts zu essen zu Hause.
It was her <u>plan</u> <u>to visit</u> him in May.
Sie hatte vor, ihn im Mai zu besuchen.

- bestimmten **Adjektiven** (auch in Verbindung mit *too/enough*) und deren Steigerungsformen, z. B.:

certain	sicher
difficult/hard	schwer, schwierig
easy	leicht

It was <u>difficult</u> <u>to follow</u> her.
Es war schwer, ihr zu folgen.

- **Fragewörtern**, wie z. B. *what, where, which, who, when, how* und nach *whether*. Diese Konstruktion ersetzt eine indirekte Frage mit modalem Hilfsverb.

We knew <u>where</u> <u>to find</u> her. /
We knew <u>where</u> <u>we</u> <u>would find</u> her.
Wir wussten, wo wir sie finden würden.

Die Konstruktion **Objekt + Infinitiv** wird im Deutschen oft mit einem „dass"-Satz übersetzt.
Sie steht z. B. **nach**
- bestimmten **Verben**, z. B.:

to allow	erlauben
to get	veranlassen
to help	helfen
to persuade	überreden

She <u>allowed</u> <u>him</u> <u>to go</u> to the cinema.
Sie erlaubte ihm, dass er ins Kino geht. / ... ins Kino zu gehen.

- **Verb + Präposition**, z. B.:

to count on	rechnen mit
to rely on	sich verlassen auf
to wait for	warten auf

She <u>relies on</u> <u>him</u> <u>to arrive</u> in time.
Sie verlässt sich darauf, dass er rechtzeitig ankommt.

- **Adjektiv + Präposition**, z. B.:

easy for	leicht
necessary for	notwendig
nice of	nett
silly of	dumm

It is <u>necessary</u> <u>for you</u> <u>to learn</u> maths.
Es ist notwendig, dass du Mathe lernst.

- **Substantiv + Präposition**, z. B.:

opportunity for	Gelegenheit
idea for	Idee
time for	Zeit
mistake for	Fehler

Work experience is a good <u>opportunity</u> <u>for you</u> <u>to find out</u> which job suits you.
Ein Praktikum ist eine gute Gelegenheit, herauszufinden, welcher Beruf zu dir passt.

- einem **Adjektiv**, das durch *too* oder *enough* näher bestimmt wird.

The box is <u>too</u> <u>heavy</u> <u>for me</u> <u>to carry</u>.
Die Kiste ist mir zu schwer zum Tragen.
The weather is <u>good</u> <u>enough</u> <u>for us</u> <u>to go</u> for a walk. *Das Wetter ist gut genug, dass wir spazieren gehen können.*

7 Gerundium (*-ing*-Form) – *Gerund*

Bildung
Infinitiv + *-ing*

read → read<u>ing</u>

G 11

Beachte:
- stummes *-e* entfällt
- nach kurzem betontem Vokal: Schlusskonsonant verdoppelt
- *-ie* wird zu *-y*

write → writing
stop → stopping

lie → lying

Verwendung
Die *-ing*-Form steht nach bestimmten Ausdrücken und kann verschiedene Funktionen im Satz einnehmen, z. B.:

- als **Subjekt** des Satzes

  Skiing is fun. *Skifahren macht Spaß.*

- nach bestimmten **Verben** (als **Objekt** des Satzes), z. B.:
to avoid	vermeiden
to enjoy	genießen, gern tun
to keep (on)	weitermachen
to miss	vermissen
to risk	riskieren
to suggest	vorschlagen

  He enjoys reading comics.
  Er liest gerne Comics.

  You risk losing a friend.
  Du riskierst, einen Freund zu verlieren.

- nach **Verb + Präposition**, z. B.:
to agree with	zustimmen
to believe in	glauben an
to dream of	träumen von
to look forward to	sich freuen auf
to talk about	sprechen über

  She dreams of meeting a star.
  Sie träumt davon, einen Star zu treffen.

- nach **Adjektiv + Präposition**, z. B.:
afraid of	sich fürchten vor
famous for	berühmt für
good/bad at	gut/schlecht in
interested in	interessiert an

  He is afraid of losing his job.
  Er hat Angst, seine Arbeit zu verlieren.

- nach **Substantiv + Präposition**, z. B.:
chance of	Chance, Aussicht
danger of	Gefahr
reason for	Grund
way of	Art und Weise

  Do you have a chance of getting the job?
  Hast du Aussicht, die Stelle zu bekommen?

- nach **Präpositionen** und **Konjunktionen der Zeit**, z. B.:

after	nachdem
before	bevor
by	indem, dadurch, dass
in spite of	trotz
instead of	statt

Before leaving the room he said goodbye.
Bevor er den Raum verließ, verabschiedete er sich.

8 Infinitiv oder Gerundium? – *Infinitive or Gerund?*

Einige Verben können sowohl **mit dem Infinitiv** als auch **mit der -ing-Form** stehen, **ohne** dass sich die **Bedeutung ändert**, z. B.
to love, to hate, to prefer, to start, to begin, to continue.

I hate getting up early.
I hate to get up early.
Ich hasse es, früh aufzustehen.

Bei manchen Verben **ändert sich** jedoch die **Bedeutung**, je nachdem, ob sie mit Infinitiv oder mit der -*ing*-Form verwendet werden, z. B. *to remember, to forget, to stop.*

- *to remember* + Infinitiv:
  „daran denken, etwas zu tun"

  I must remember to post the invitations.
  Ich muss daran denken, die Einladungen einzuwerfen.

  to remember + *ing*-Form:
  „sich erinnern, etwas getan zu haben"

  I remember posting the invitations.
  Ich erinnere mich daran, die Einladungen eingeworfen zu haben.

- *to forget* + Infinitiv:
  „vergessen, etwas zu tun"

  Don't forget to water the plants.
  Vergiss nicht, die Pflanzen zu gießen.

  to forget + *ing*-Form:
  „vergessen, etwas getan zu haben"

  I'll never forget meeting the President.
  Ich werde nie vergessen, wie ich den Präsidenten traf.

- *to stop* + Infinitiv:
  „stehen bleiben, um etwas zu tun"

  I stopped to read the road sign.
  Ich hielt an, um das Verkehrsschild zu lesen.

  to stop + *ing*-Form:
  „aufhören, etwas zu tun"

  He stopped laughing.
  Er hörte auf zu lachen.

9 Partizipien – *Participles*

Partizip Präsens – *Present Participle*

Bildung
Infinitiv + *ing*
Sonderformen: siehe *gerund*
(S. G 11 f.)

talk → talking

Verwendung
Das *present participle* verwendet man:
- zur Bildung der Verlaufsform *present progressive*,
- zur Bildung der Verlaufsform *past progressive*,
- zur Bildung der Verlaufsform *present perfect progressive*,
- zur Bildung der Verlaufsform *future progressive*,
- wie ein Adjektiv, wenn es vor einem Substantiv steht.

Peter is reading.
Peter liest (gerade).

Peter was reading when I saw him.
Peter las (gerade), als ich ihn sah.

I have been living in Sydney for 5 years.
Ich lebe seit 5 Jahren in Sydney.

This time tomorrow I will be working.
Morgen um diese Zeit werde ich arbeiten.

The village hasn't got running water.
Das Dorf hat kein fließendes Wasser.

Partizip Perfekt – *Past Participle*

Bildung
Infinitiv + *-ed*

Beachte:
- stummes *-e* entfällt
- nach kurzem betontem Vokal wird der Schlusskonsonant verdoppelt
- *-y* wird zu *-ie*
- unregelmäßige Verben (S. G 31 f.)

talk → talked

live → lived
stop → stopped

cry → cried
be → been

Verwendung
Das *past participle* verwendet man
- zur Bildung des *present perfect*,

He hasn't talked to Tom yet.
Er hat noch nicht mit Tom gesprochen.

• zur Bildung des *past perfect*,	Before they went biking in France, they had <u>bought</u> new bikes. *Bevor sie nach Frankreich zum Radfahren gingen, hatten sie neue Fahrräder gekauft.*
• zur Bildung des *future perfect*,	The letter will have <u>arrived</u> by then. *Der Brief wird bis dann angekommen sein.*
• zur Bildung des Passivs,	The fish was <u>eaten</u> by the cat. *Der Fisch wurde von der Katze gefressen.*
• wie ein Adjektiv, wenn es vor einem Substantiv steht.	Peter has got a well-<u>paid</u> job. *Peter hat eine gut bezahlte Stelle.*

Verkürzung eines Nebensatzes durch ein Partizip

Adverbiale Nebensätze (meist kausale oder temporale Bedeutung) und **Relativsätze** können durch ein Partizip verkürzt werden.

She watches the news, because she wants to stay informed.
<u>Wanting</u> to stay informed, she watches the news.
Sie sieht sich die Nachrichten an, weil sie informiert bleiben möchte.

Aus der Zeitform des Verbs im Nebensatz ergibt sich, welches Partizip für die Satzverkürzung verwendet wird:

- Steht das Verb im Nebensatz im *present* oder *past tense* (*simple* und *progressive form*), verwendet man das *present participle*.

he finishes
he finished } → finishing

- Steht das Verb im Nebensatz im *present perfect* oder *past perfect*, verwendet man *having + past participle*.

he has finished
he had finished } → having finished

- Das *past participle* verwendet man auch, um einen Satz im Passiv zu verkürzen.

Sally is a manager in a five-star hotel <u>which is called</u> Pacific View.
Sally is a manager in a five-star hotel <u>called</u> Pacific View.

Beachte:
- Man kann einen Temporal- oder Kausalsatz verkürzen, wenn **Haupt- und Nebensatz dasselbe Subjekt** haben.

When <u>he</u> was walking down the street, <u>he</u> saw Jo.
(When) <u>walking</u> down the street, <u>he</u> saw Jo.
Als er die Straße entlangging, sah er Jo.

G 15

- Bei **Kausalsätzen** entfallen die Konjunktionen *as, because* und *since* im verkürzten Nebensatz.
- In einem **Temporalsatz** bleibt die einleitende **Konjunktion** häufig erhalten, um dem Satz eine **eindeutige Bedeutung** zuzuweisen.

Die Vorzeitigkeit einer Handlung kann durch *after + present participle* oder durch *having + past participle* ausgedrückt werden.

- Bei **Relativsätzen** entfallen die Relativpronomen *who, which* und *that*.

As he was hungry, he bought a sandwich.
Being hungry, he bought a sandwich.
Da er hungrig war, kaufte er ein Sandwich.

When he left, he forgot to lock the door.
When leaving, he forgot to lock the door.
Als er ging, vergaß er, die Tür abzuschließen.

Tara got sick eating too much chocolate.
Tara wurde schlecht, als/während/da sie zu viel Schokolade aß.

After finishing / Having finished breakfast, he went to work.
Nachdem er sein Frühstück beendet hatte, ging er zur Arbeit.

I saw a six-year-old boy who played the piano.
I saw a six-year-old boy playing the piano.
Ich sah einen sechsjährigen Jungen, der gerade Klavier spielte. / ... Klavier spielen.

Verbindung von zwei Hauptsätzen durch ein Partizip

Zwei Hauptsätze können durch ein Partizip verbunden werden, wenn sie **dasselbe Subjekt** haben.

Beachte:
- Das Subjekt des zweiten Hauptsatzes und die Konjunktion *and* entfallen.
- Die Verbform des zweiten Hauptsatzes wird durch das Partizip ersetzt.

He did his homework and he listened to the radio.
He did his homework listening to the radio.
Er machte seine Hausaufgaben und hörte Radio.

Unverbundene Partizipialkonstruktionen – *Absolute Participle Constructions*

Unverbundene Partizipialkonstruktionen haben ein **eigenes Subjekt**, das nicht mit dem Subjekt des Hauptsatzes übereinstimmt. Sie werden in **gehobener Sprache** verwendet. Mit einleitendem *with* werden sie auf allen Stilebenen verwendet.	The <u>sun</u> having come out, the ladies went for a walk in the park. *Da die Sonne herausgekommen war, gingen die Damen im Park spazieren.* With the <u>telephone</u> ringing, she jumped out of bed. *Als das Telefon klingelte, sprang sie aus dem Bett.*

Bildung und Gebrauch der finiten Verbformen

10 Zeiten – *Tenses*

Simple Present

Bildung
Infinitiv, Ausnahme 3. Person Singular: Infinitiv + *-s*

stand – he/she/it stand<u>s</u>

Beachte:
- Bei Verben, die auf *-s, -sh, -ch, -x* und *-z* enden, wird in der 3. Person Singular *-es* angefügt.

kiss – he/she/it kiss<u>es</u>
rush – he/she/it rush<u>es</u>
teach – he/she/it teach<u>es</u>
fi<u>x</u> – he/she/it fix<u>es</u>

- Bei Verben, die auf Konsonant + *-y* enden, wird *-es* angefügt; *-y* wird zu *-i-*.

carry – he/she/it carr<u>ies</u>

Bildung von Fragen im *simple present*
(Fragewort +) *do/does* + Subjekt + Infinitiv

Where <u>does</u> he <u>live</u>? / <u>Does</u> he <u>live</u> in London?
Wo lebt er? / Lebt er in London?

Beachte:
Die Umschreibung mit *do/does* wird nicht verwendet,
- wenn nach dem Subjekt gefragt wird (mit *who, what, which*),

Who <u>likes</u> pizza?
Wer mag Pizza?
<u>Which</u> tree <u>has</u> more leaves?
Welcher Baum hat mehr Blätter?

- wenn die Frage mit *is/are* gebildet wird.

<u>Are</u> you happy?
Bist du glücklich?

Bildung der Verneinung im *simple present*
don't/doesn't + Infinitiv

He doesn't like football.
Er mag Fußball nicht.

Verwendung
Das *simple present* wird verwendet:
- bei Tätigkeiten, die man **gewohnheitsmäßig** oder häufig ausführt
  Signalwörter: z. B. *always, often, never, every day, every morning, every afternoon*
- bei **allgemeingültigen** Aussagen
- bei **Zustandsverben**: Sie drücken Eigenschaften / Zustände von Personen und Dingen aus und stehen normalerweise nur in der *simple form*, z. B. *to hate, to know, to like*.

Every morning John buys a newspaper.
Jeden Morgen kauft John eine Zeitung.

London is a big city.
London ist eine große Stadt.

I like science-fiction films.
Ich mag Science-Fiction-Filme.

Present Progressive / Present Continuous

Bildung
am/is/are + *present participle*

read → am/is/are reading

Bildung von Fragen im *present progressive*
(Fragewort +) *am/is/are* + Subjekt + *present participle*

Is Peter reading? / What is he reading?
Liest Peter gerade? / Was liest er?

Bildung der Verneinung im *present progressive*
am not/isn't/aren't + *present participle*

Peter isn't reading.
Peter liest gerade nicht.

Verwendung
Mit dem *present progressive* drückt man aus, dass etwas **gerade passiert** und **noch nicht abgeschlossen** ist. Es wird daher auch als **Verlaufsform** der Gegenwart bezeichnet.

Signalwörter: *at the moment, now*

At the moment, Peter is drinking a cup of tea.
Im Augenblick trinkt Peter eine Tasse Tee.
[Er hat damit angefangen und noch nicht aufgehört.]

Simple Past

Bildung
Regelmäßige Verben: Infinitiv + *-ed*

Beachte:
- stummes *-e* entfällt
- Bei Verben, die auf Konsonant + *-y* enden, wird *-y* zu *-i-*.
- Nach kurzem betontem Vokal wird der Schlusskonsonant verdoppelt.

Unregelmäßige Verben: siehe Liste S. G 31 f.

walk → walk<u>ed</u>

hop<u>e</u> → hop<u>ed</u>
car<u>ry</u> → carr<u>ied</u>

st<u>o</u>p → sto<u>pped</u>

be → was
have → had

Bildung von Fragen im *simple past*
(Fragewort +) *did* + Subjekt + Infinitiv

(<u>Why</u>) <u>Did</u> <u>he</u> <u>look</u> out of the window?
(Warum) Sah er aus dem Fenster?

Beachte:
Die Umschreibung mit *did* wird nicht verwendet,
- wenn nach dem Subjekt gefragt wird (mit *who, what, which*),

<u>Who</u> <u>paid</u> the bill?
Wer zahlte die Rechnung?

<u>What</u> <u>happened</u> to your friend?
Was ist mit deinem Freund passiert?

- wenn die Frage mit *was/were* gebildet wird.

<u>Were</u> you happy?
Warst du glücklich?

Bildung der Verneinung im *simple past*
didn't + Infinitiv

He <u>didn't</u> <u>call</u> me.
Er rief mich nicht an.

Verwendung
Das *simple past* beschreibt Handlungen und Ereignisse, die **in der Vergangenheit passierten** und **bereits abgeschlossen** sind.

Signalwörter: z. B. *yesterday, last week/year, two years ago, in 2008*

Last week, he <u>helped</u> me with my homework.
Letzte Woche half er mir bei meinen Hausaufgaben. [Die Handlung fand in der letzten Woche statt, ist also abgeschlossen.]

Past Progressive / Past Continuous

Bildung
was/were + present participle

watch → was/were watching

Verwendung
Die **Verlaufsform** *past progressive* verwendet man, wenn **zu einem bestimmten Zeitpunkt** in der Vergangenheit eine **Handlung ablief**, bzw. wenn eine **Handlung** von einer anderen **unterbrochen** wurde.

Yesterday at 9 o'clock I was still sleeping.
Gestern um 9 Uhr schlief ich noch.
I was reading a book when Peter came into the room.
Ich las (gerade) ein Buch, als Peter ins Zimmer kam.

Present Perfect (Simple)

Bildung
have/has + past participle

write → has/have written

Verwendung
Das *present perfect* verwendet man,
- wenn ein Vorgang **in der Vergangenheit begonnen** hat und **noch andauert**,
- wenn das Ergebnis einer vergangenen Handlung **Auswirkungen auf die Gegenwart** hat.

Signalwörter: z. B. *already, ever, just, how long, not ... yet, since, for*

Beachte:
- *have/has* können zu *'ve/'s* verkürzt werden.
- Das *present perfect* wird oft mit *since* und *for* verwendet („seit").
  - *since* gibt einen **Zeitpunkt** an:

  - *for* gibt einen **Zeitraum** an:

He has lived in London since 2008.
Er lebt seit 2008 in London.
[Er lebt jetzt immer noch in London.]
I have just cleaned my car.
Ich habe gerade mein Auto geputzt.
[Man sieht evtl. das saubere Auto.]
Have you ever been to Dublin?
Warst du schon jemals in Dublin?

He's given me his umbrella.
Er hat mir seinen Regenschirm gegeben.

Ron has lived in Sydney since 2007.
Ron lebt seit 2007 in Sydney.

Sally has lived in Berlin for five years.
Sally lebt seit fünf Jahren in Berlin.

Present Perfect Progressive / Present Perfect Continuous

Bildung
have/has + been + present participle

write → has/have been writing

Verwendung
Die **Verlaufsform** *present perfect progressive* verwendet man, um die **Dauer einer Handlung** zu **betonen**, die in der Vergangenheit begonnen hat und noch andauert.

She has been sleeping for ten hours.
Sie schläft seit zehn Stunden.

Past Perfect (Simple)

Bildung
had + past participle

write → had written

Verwendung
Die Vorvergangenheit *past perfect* verwendet man, wenn ein Vorgang in der Vergangenheit **vor einem anderen Vorgang in der Vergangenheit abgeschlossen** wurde.

He had bought a ticket before he took the train to Manchester.
Er hatte eine Fahrkarte gekauft, bevor er den Zug nach Manchester nahm. [Beim Einsteigen war der Kauf abgeschlossen.]

Past Perfect Progressive / Past Perfect Continuous

Bildung
had + been + present participle

write → had been writing

Verwendung
Die **Verlaufsform** *past perfect progressive* verwendet man für **Handlungen**, die in der Vergangenheit **bis zu dem Zeitpunkt andauerten**, zu dem eine neue Handlung einsetzte.

She had been sleeping for ten hours when the doorbell rang.
Sie hatte seit zehn Stunden geschlafen, als es an der Tür klingelte. [Das Schlafen dauerte bis zu dem Zeitpunkt an, als es an der Tür klingelte.]

Will-future

Bildung
will + Infinitiv

buy → <u>will</u> <u>buy</u>

Bildung von Fragen im
will-future
(Fragewort +) *will* + Subjekt +
Infinitiv

<u>What</u> <u>will</u> y<u>ou</u> <u>buy</u>?
Was wirst du kaufen?

Bildung der Verneinung im
will-future
won't + Infinitiv

Why <u>won't</u> you <u>come</u> to our party?
Warum kommst du nicht zu unserer Party?

Verwendung
Das *will-future* verwendet man, wenn ein Vorgang **in der Zukunft stattfinden** wird:
- bei Vorhersagen oder Vermutungen,
- bei spontanen Entscheidungen.

The weather <u>will</u> <u>be</u> fine tomorrow.
Das Wetter wird morgen schön (sein).
[doorbell] "I'<u>ll</u> <u>open</u> the door."
"Ich werde die Tür öffnen."

Signalwörter: z. B. *tomorrow, next week, next Monday, next year, in three years, soon*

Going-to-future

Bildung
am/is/are + *going to* + Infinitiv

find → <u>am/is/are</u> <u>going to</u> <u>find</u>

Verwendung
Das *going-to-future* verwendet man, wenn man ausdrücken will:
- was man für die Zukunft **plant** oder **zu tun beabsichtigt**.

- dass ein **Ereignis bald eintreten wird**, da bestimmte **Anzeichen** vorhanden sind.

I <u>am going to work</u> in England this summer.
Diesen Sommer werde ich in England arbeiten.

Look at those clouds. It's <u>going to rain</u> soon.
Schau dir diese Wolken an. Es wird bald regnen.

Simple Present und Present Progressive zur Wiedergabe der Zukunft

Verwendung
- Mit dem *present progressive* drückt man **Pläne** für die Zukunft aus, für die bereits **Vorkehrungen** getroffen wurden.
- Mit dem *simple present* wird ein zukünftiges Geschehen wiedergegeben, das **von außen festgelegt** wurde, z. B. Fahrpläne, Programme, Kalender.

We <u>are fly</u>ing to New York tomorrow.
Morgen fliegen wir nach New York.
[Wir haben schon Tickets.]

The train <u>leaves</u> at 8.15 a.m.
Der Zug fährt um 8.15 Uhr.
The play <u>ends</u> at 10 p.m.
Das Theaterstück endet um 22 Uhr.

Future Progressive / Future Continuous

Bildung
will + be + present participle

work → <u>will</u> <u>be</u> <u>working</u>

Verwendung
Die **Verlaufsform** *future progressive* drückt aus, dass ein **Vorgang** in der Zukunft zu einem bestimmten Zeitpunkt **gerade ablaufen wird**.

Signalwörter: *this time next week / tomorrow, tomorrow* + Zeitangabe

This time tomorrow I <u>will</u> <u>be</u> <u>sitting</u> in a plane to London.
Morgen um diese Zeit werde ich gerade im Flugzeug nach London sitzen.

Future Perfect (Future II)

Bildung
will + have + past participle

go → <u>will</u> <u>have</u> <u>gone</u>

Verwendung
Das *future perfect* drückt aus, dass ein **Vorgang** in der Zukunft **abgeschlossen sein wird** (Vorzeitigkeit in der Zukunft).

Signalwörter: *by then, by* + Zeitangabe

By 5 p.m. tomorrow I <u>will</u> <u>have</u> <u>arrived</u> in London.
Morgen Nachmittag um fünf Uhr werde ich bereits in London angekommen sein.

11 Passiv – *Passive Voice*

Bildung
Form von *(to) be* in der entsprechenden Zeitform + *past participle*

The bridge <u>was</u> <u>finished</u> in 1894.
Die Brücke wurde 1894 fertiggestellt.

Zeitformen:

- *simple present*

  Aktiv: Joe <u>buys</u> the milk.
  Passiv: The milk <u>is</u> <u>bought</u> by Joe.

- *simple past*

  Aktiv: Joe <u>bought</u> the milk.
  Passiv: The milk <u>was</u> <u>bought</u> by Joe.

- *present perfect*

  Aktiv: Joe <u>has bought</u> the milk.
  Passiv: The milk <u>has been</u> <u>bought</u> by Joe.

- *past perfect*

  Aktiv: Joe <u>had bought</u> the milk.
  Passiv: The milk <u>had been</u> <u>bought</u> by Joe.

- *will-future*

  Aktiv: Joe <u>will buy</u> the milk.
  Passiv: The milk <u>will be</u> <u>bought</u> by Joe.

- *future perfect (future II)*

  Aktiv: Joe <u>will have bought</u> the milk.
  Passiv: The milk <u>will have been</u> <u>bought</u> by Joe.

- *conditional I*

  Aktiv: Joe <u>would buy</u> the milk.
  Passiv: The milk <u>would be</u> <u>bought</u> by Joe.

- *conditional II*

  Aktiv: Joe <u>would have bought</u> the milk.
  Passiv: The milk <u>would have been</u> <u>bought</u> by Joe.

Aktiv → Passiv

- Das Subjekt des Aktivsatzes wird zum Objekt des Passivsatzes. Es wird mit *by* angeschlossen.
- Das Objekt des Aktivsatzes wird zum Subjekt des Passivsatzes.

Aktiv: <u>Joe</u> buys <u>the milk</u>.
       Subjekt   Objekt

Passiv: <u>The milk</u> is bought <u>by Joe</u>.
        Subjekt   by-agent

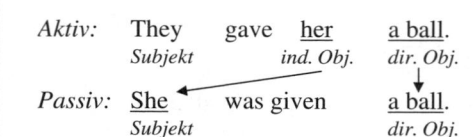

- Stehen im Aktiv **zwei Objekte**, lassen sich zwei verschiedene Passivsätze bilden. Ein Objekt wird zum Subjekt des Passivsatzes, das zweite bleibt Objekt.

Aktiv: They gave <u>her</u> <u>a ball</u>.
       Subjekt ind. Obj. dir. Obj.

Passiv: <u>She</u> was given <u>a ball</u>.
        Subjekt   dir. Obj.

oder:

Aktiv: They gave <u>her</u> <u>a ball</u>.
       Subjekt ind. Obj. dir. Obj.

Passiv: <u>A ball</u> was given <u>to her</u>.
        Subjekt   ind. Obj.

Beachte:
Das indirekte Objekt muss im Passivsatz mit *to* angeschlossen werden.

Passiv → Aktiv
- Der mit *by* angeschlossene Handelnde *(by-agent)* des Passivsatzes wird zum Subjekt des Aktivsatzes; *by* entfällt.
- Das Subjekt des Passivsatzes wird zum Objekt des Aktivsatzes.
- Fehlt im Passivsatz der *by-agent*, muss im Aktivsatz ein Handelnder als Subjekt ergänzt werden, z. B. *somebody, we, you, they*.

Passiv: The milk is bought by Joe.
 Subjekt *by-agent*
Aktiv: Joe ← buys → the milk.
 Subjekt *Objekt*

Passiv: The match was won.
 Subjekt
Aktiv: They won the match.
 (ergänztes) *Objekt*
 Subjekt

Der Satz im Englischen

12 Wortstellung – *Word Order*

Im Aussagesatz gilt die Wortstellung
<u>S</u>ubjekt – <u>P</u>rädikat – <u>O</u>bjekt
(subject – verb – object):
- <u>Subjekt</u>: Wer oder was tut etwas?
- <u>Prädikat</u>: Was wird getan?
- <u>Objekt</u>: Worauf/Auf wen bezieht sich die Tätigkeit?

Für die Position von Orts- und Zeitangaben vgl. S. G 4 f.

Cats catch mice.
Katzen fangen Mäuse.

13 Konditionalsätze – *Conditional Sentences*

Ein Konditionalsatz (Bedingungssatz) besteht aus zwei Teilen: einem Nebensatz *(if-clause)* und einem Hauptsatz *(main clause)*. Im *if*-Satz steht die **Bedingung** *(condition)*, unter der die im **Hauptsatz** genannte **Folge** eintritt. Man unterscheidet drei Arten von Konditionalsätzen:

Konditionalsatz Typ I

Bildung
- *if*-Satz (Bedingung):
  simple present
- Hauptsatz (Folge):
  will-future

Der *if*-Satz kann auch nach dem Hauptsatz stehen. In diesem Fall entfällt das Komma:
- Hauptsatz: *will-future*

- *if*-Satz: *simple present*

Im Hauptsatz kann auch
- *can* + Infinitiv,

- *must* + Infinitiv,

- der Imperativ
stehen.

If you read this book,
Wenn du dieses Buch liest,
you will learn a lot about music.
erfährst du eine Menge über Musik.

You will learn a lot about music
Du erfährst eine Menge über Musik,
if you read this book.
wenn du dieses Buch liest.

If you go to London, you can see Bob.
Wenn du nach London fährst, kannst du Bob treffen.

If you go to London, you must visit me.
Wenn du nach London fährst, musst du mich besuchen.

If it rains, take an umbrella.
Wenn es regnet, nimm einen Schirm mit.

Verwendung
Bedingungssätze vom Typ I verwendet man, wenn die **Bedingung erfüllbar** ist. Man gibt an, was unter bestimmten Bedingungen **geschieht** oder **geschehen kann**.

Konditionalsatz Typ II

Bildung
- *if*-Satz (Bedingung):
  simple past
- Hauptsatz (Folge):
  conditional I = would + Infinitiv

If I went to London,
Wenn ich nach London fahren würde,
I would visit the Tower.
würde ich mir den Tower ansehen.

Verwendung
Bedingungssätze vom Typ II verwendet man, wenn die **Bedingung nur theoretisch erfüllt** werden kann oder **nicht erfüllbar** ist.

Konditionalsatz Typ III

Bildung
- *if*-Satz (Bedingung): *past perfect*
- Hauptsatz (Folge): *conditional II = would + have + past participle*

If I had gone to London,
Wenn ich nach London gefahren wäre,
I would have visited the Tower of London.
hätte ich mir den Tower of London angesehen.

Verwendung
Bedingungssätze vom Typ III verwendet man, wenn sich die **Bedingung auf die Vergangenheit bezieht** und deshalb **nicht mehr erfüllbar** ist.

14 Relativsätze – *Relative Clauses*

Ein Relativsatz ist ein Nebensatz, der sich **auf eine Person oder Sache** des Hauptsatzes **bezieht** und diese **näher beschreibt**:
- Hauptsatz:
- Relativsatz:

The boy who looks like Jane is her brother.
Der Junge, der Jane ähnlich sieht, ist ihr Bruder.

The boy ... is her brother.
... who looks like Jane ...

Bildung
Haupt- und Nebensatz werden durch das Relativpronomen verbunden.
- ***who*** (Nominativ oder Akkusativ),

Peter, who lives in London, likes travelling.
Peter, der in London lebt, reist gerne.

G 27

whose (Genitiv) und

whom (Akkusativ) beziehen sich auf **Personen**,

- *which* bezieht sich auf **Sachen**,

- *that* kann sich auf **Sachen** und auf **Personen** beziehen und wird nur verwendet, wenn die **Information** im Relativsatz **notwendig** ist, um den ganzen Satz zu verstehen.

Sam, whose mother is an architect, is in my class.
Sam, dessen Mutter Architektin ist, geht in meine Klasse.
Anne, whom/who I like very much, is French.
Anne, die ich sehr mag, ist Französin.
The film "Dark Moon", which we saw yesterday, was far too long.
Der Film „Dark Moon", den wir gestern sahen, war viel zu lang.
The film that we saw last week was much better.
Der Film, den wir letzte Woche sahen, war viel besser.

Verwendung
Mithilfe von Relativpronomen kann man **zwei Sätze miteinander verbinden**.

London is England's biggest city. London has about 7.2 million inhabitants.
London ist Englands größte Stadt. London hat etwa 7,2 Millionen Einwohner.
London, which is England's biggest city, has about 7.2 million inhabitants.
London, die größte Stadt Englands, hat etwa 7,2 Millionen Einwohner.

Beachte:
Man unterscheidet zwei Arten von Relativsätzen:
- **Notwendige Relativsätze** *(defining relative clauses)* enthalten Informationen, die **für das Verständnis** des Satzes **erforderlich** sind.

  Hier kann das Relativpronomen entfallen, wenn es Objekt ist; man spricht dann auch von *contact clauses*.

The man who is wearing a red shirt is Mike.
Der Mann, der ein rotes Hemd trägt, ist Mike.

The book (that) I bought yesterday is thrilling.
Das Buch, das ich gestern gekauft habe, ist spannend.

- **Nicht notwendige Relativsätze** *(non-defining relative clauses)* enthalten **zusätzliche Informationen** zum Bezugswort, die für das Verständnis des Satzes nicht unbedingt notwendig sind. Dieser Typ von Relativsatz wird **mit Komma** abgetrennt.

Sally, who went to a party yesterday, is very tired.
Sally, die gestern auf einer Party war, ist sehr müde.

15 Indirekte Rede – *Reported Speech*

Die indirekte Rede verwendet man, um **wiederzugeben, was ein anderer gesagt** oder **gefragt hat**.

Bildung
Um die indirekte Rede zu bilden, benötigt man ein **Einleitungsverb**. Häufig verwendete Einleitungsverben sind:

to say, to tell, to add, to mention, to think, to ask, to want to know, to answer

In der indirekten Rede verändern sich die **Pronomen**, in bestimmten Fällen auch die **Zeiten** und die **Orts-** und **Zeitangaben**.

- Wie die Pronomen sich verändern, hängt vom jeweiligen **Kontext** ab.

direkte Rede	indirekte Rede
Bob says to Jenny: "I like y<u>ou</u>." *Bob sagt zu Jenny: „Ich mag dich."*	Jenny tells Liz: "Bob says that he likes <u>me</u>." *Jenny erzählt Liz: „Bob sagt, dass er mich mag."*
Aber:	Jenny tells Liz that Bob likes <u>her</u>. *Jenny erzählt Liz, dass Bob sie mag.*

- **Zeiten**: Keine Veränderung, wenn das Einleitungsverb im *simple present* oder im *present perfect* steht:

direkte Rede	indirekte Rede
Bob <u>says</u>, "I <u>love</u> dancing." *Bob sagt: „Ich tanze sehr gerne."*	Bob <u>says</u> (that) he <u>loves</u> dancing. *Bob sagt, er tanze sehr gerne.*

In folgenden Fällen wird die Zeit der direkten Rede in der indirekten Rede **um eine Zeitstufe zurückversetzt**, wenn das **Einleitungsverb** im *simple past* steht:

simple present	→	*simple past*
simple past	→	*past perfect*
present perfect	→	*past perfect*
will-future	→	*conditional I*

- **Zeitangaben** verändern sich, wenn der Bericht zu einem späteren Zeitpunkt erfolgt, z. B.:
- Welche **Ortsangabe** verwendet wird, hängt davon ab, wo sich der Sprecher im Moment befindet.

Bob said, "I love dancing."
Bob sagte: „Ich tanze sehr gerne."

Joe: "I like it."
Joe: "I liked it."

Joe: "I've liked it."

Joe: "I will like it."

now	→	then, at that time
today	→	that day, yesterday
yesterday	→	the day before
the day before yesterday	→	two days before
tomorrow	→	the following day
next week	→	the following week
here	→	there

Bob said (that) he loved dancing.
Bob sagte, er tanze sehr gerne.

Joe said he liked it.
Joe said he had liked it.

Joe said he had liked it.

Joe said he would like it.

Bildung der indirekten Frage
Häufige Einleitungsverben für die indirekte Frage sind:

- **Fragewörter** bleiben in der indirekten Rede **erhalten**. Die **Umschreibung** mit *do/does/did* **entfällt** in der indirekten Frage.

- Enthält die direkte Frage **kein Fragewort**, wird die indirekte Frage mit *whether* oder *if* eingeleitet:

to ask, to want to know, to wonder

Tom: "When did they arrive?"
Tom: „Wann sind sie angekommen?"

Tom: "Are they staying at the hotel?"
Tom: „Übernachten sie im Hotel?"

Tom asked when they had arrived.
Tom fragte, wann sie angekommen seien.

Tom asked if/ whether they were staying at the hotel.
Tom fragte, ob sie im Hotel übernachten.

Befehle/Aufforderungen in der indirekten Rede
Häufige Einleitungsverben sind:
In der indirekten Rede steht hier **Einleitungsverb + Objekt + (not) to + Infinitiv**.

to tell, to order, to ask

Tom: "Leave the room."
Tom: „Verlass den Raum."

Tom told me to leave the room.
Tom forderte mich auf, den Raum zu verlassen.

Anhang

16 Liste wichtiger unregelmäßiger Verben – *List of Irregular Verbs*

Infinitive	Simple Past	Past Participle	*Deutsch*
be	was/were	been	*sein*
begin	began	begun	*beginnen*
blow	blew	blown	*wehen, blasen*
break	broke	broken	*brechen*
bring	brought	brought	*bringen*
build	built	built	*bauen*
buy	bought	bought	*kaufen*
catch	caught	caught	*fangen*
choose	chose	chosen	*wählen*
come	came	come	*kommen*
cut	cut	cut	*schneiden*
do	did	done	*tun*
draw	drew	drawn	*zeichnen*
drink	drank	drunk	*trinken*
drive	drove	driven	*fahren*
eat	ate	eaten	*essen*
fall	fell	fallen	*fallen*
feed	fed	fed	*füttern*
feel	felt	felt	*fühlen*
find	found	found	*finden*
fly	flew	flown	*fliegen*
get	got	got	*bekommen*
give	gave	given	*geben*
go	went	gone	*gehen*
grow	grew	grown	*wachsen*
hang	hung	hung	*hängen*
have	had	had	*haben*
hear	heard	heard	*hören*
hit	hit	hit	*schlagen*
hold	held	held	*halten*
keep	kept	kept	*halten*
know	knew	known	*wissen*

Infinitive	Simple Past	Past Participle	*Deutsch*
lay	laid	laid	*legen*
leave	left	left	*verlassen*
let	let	let	*lassen*
lie	lay	lain	*liegen*
lose	lost	lost	*verlieren*
make	made	made	*machen*
meet	met	met	*treffen*
pay	paid	paid	*bezahlen*
put	put	put	*stellen/setzen*
read	read	read	*lesen*
ring	rang	rung	*läuten/anrufen*
run	ran	run	*rennen*
say	said	said	*sagen*
see	saw	seen	*sehen*
send	sent	sent	*schicken*
show	showed	shown	*zeigen*
sing	sang	sung	*singen*
sit	sat	sat	*sitzen*
sleep	slept	slept	*schlafen*
smell	smelt	smelt	*riechen*
speak	spoke	spoken	*sprechen*
spend	spent	spent	*ausgeben/ verbringen*
stand	stood	stood	*stehen*
steal	stole	stolen	*stehlen*
swim	swam	swum	*schwimmen*
take	took	taken	*nehmen*
teach	taught	taught	*lehren*
tell	told	told	*erzählen*
think	thought	thought	*denken*
throw	threw	thrown	*werfen*
wake	woke	woken	*aufwachen*
wear	wore	worn	*tragen*
win	won	won	*gewinnen*
write	wrote	written	*schreiben*

Schriftliche Prüfung zum Mittleren Schulabschluss in Berlin
Englisch 2012

Listening Part 1: Conversations

- You are going to hear four short conversations.
- You will hear the recording twice.
- Match each conversation (1–4) with the correct picture (A–F) and put a tick (✓) in the box.
- There are two pictures that you do not need.

2012-1

Number		A	B	C	D	E	F
1	Conversation 1						
2	Conversation 2						
3	Conversation 3						
4	Conversation 4						

Listening Part 2: Radio Ads

Please note: You do not need to understand every word to do this task.
- You are going to listen to four radio ads (ads 1–4).
- You will hear the recording twice.
- Read the statements below first, then listen to the recording.
- For each ad choose the correct statement (A–C) and put a tick (✓) in the right box.
- There is only one correct statement for each ad.

5. **(Ad 1)**
   This radio ad tells you about a new program which …
   A ☐ helps to stop young people from dropping out of school.
   B ☐ offers free transport for Mississippi kids.
   C ☐ helps Mississippi kids with their maths problems.

6. **(Ad 2)**
   This radio ad tells South Africans that they should …
   A ☐ learn to play an instrument.
   B ☐ take part in writing classes.
   C ☐ identify with their country.

7. **(Ad 3)**
   This radio ad tells you …
   A ☐ to make sure that nobody gets hold of your personal information.
   B ☐ that there is a hotline which helps citizens with money problems.
   C ☐ that there is an organization that trains dogs to find criminals.

8. **(Ad 4)**
   In this radio ad London citizens are asked to …
   A ☐ smile more on public transport.
   B ☐ report any accidents at once.
   C ☐ report anything unusual.

Listening Part 3: Ellis Island

- You are going to hear an audio tour.
- You will hear the recording twice.
- Read the ten statements below first, then listen to the recording.
- If you think a statement is correct, put a tick (✓) in the box for **YES**.
- If you think a statement is not correct, put a tick (✓) in the box for **NO**.

		Yes	No
9.	The immigration center on Ellis Island was open from 1892 to 1954.	☐	☐
10.	Annie's journey took more than two weeks.	☐	☐
11.	Annie left Ireland to join her parents in America.	☐	☐
12.	Annie was unsure about her future life in America.	☐	☐
13.	Annie did not mind the terrible conditions on the ship.	☐	☐
14.	Annie's brothers fell seriously ill during the journey to America.	☐	☐
15.	On the ship, the passengers prepared for the immigration interviews.	☐	☐
16.	The sight of the Statue of Liberty made Annie speechless.	☐	☐
17.	When Annie left the ship, she got a birthday present.	☐	☐
18.	The story of Annie and her brothers is a sad one.	☐	☐

Listening Part 4: CouchSurfing

- You are going to hear a radio show about Couch-Surfing.
- There are four people in the show: the presenter Vincent Canary and three guests: Dido Bransted, her mother Linda and the CouchSurfer Jonathan Wilder.
- You will hear the recording twice.

- Read the statements below first, then listen to the recording.
- Put a tick (✓) in the box next to the correct statement.
- Only one statement is correct in each case.

19. In this show you can
    A ☐ find out about a special way of travelling.
    B ☐ win a summer holiday in a European country.
    C ☐ both A + B

20. The experiences Jonathan had as a CouchSurfer
    A ☐ were turned into a film.
    B ☐ helped him at school.
    C ☐ changed his view of the world.

21. On the CouchSurfing website you can find
    A ☐ people who offer a place to stay.
    B ☐ details about flights and trains.
    C ☐ both A + B

22. In order to make sure that CouchSurfers travel safely, they should
    A ☐ get in touch with their host's neighbours.
    B ☐ publish their experiences on the website.
    C ☐ take part in a CouchSurfing safety course.

23. To thank the hosts for their friendliness, CouchSurfers
    A ☐ must also offer a place to stay at their home.
    B ☐ must invite the hosts to a restaurant.
    C ☐ do not have to pay the hosts.

24. The most important idea behind CouchSurfing is to
    A ☐ show young people the famous sights of the world.
    B ☐ help people understand other cultures.
    C ☐ both A + B

25. At the end of the first part of the show,
    A ☐ Dido suggests going CouchSurfing with a grown-up.
    B ☐ Dido and her mother have not reached an agreement.
    C ☐ both A + B

Listening: Candidate Answer Sheet   Name: _____

For students: Put a tick (✓) in the correct box.

Part 1

Number		A	B	C	D	E	F
1	Con. 1						
2	Con. 2						
3	Con. 3						
4	Con. 4						

/ 4 P

Part 2

Number	A	B	C
5			
6			
7			
8			

/ 4 P

Part 3

Number	Yes	No
9		
10		
11		
12		
13		
14		
15		
16		
17		
18		

/ 10 P

Part 4

Number	A	B	C
19			
20			
21			
22			
23			
24			
25			

/ 7 P

/ 25 P

2012-5

Reading Part 1: Short Texts

- Look at the text and the statements in each task.
- What does the text say?
- Put a tick (✓) next to the statement that matches the text – **A**, **B**, **C** or **D**.
- There is only **one** correct statement for each sign.

1.
> To the Principal
>
> Madam,
>
> My daughter Sarah Hutch of class 10 has taken ill with chicken pox. Therefore, it will not be possible to send her to school for 10 days, as per physician's advice. Kindly grant her leave from 16th to 26th March 2010. I am also enclosing a medical certificate from the attending doctor.
>
> Yours faithfully,
> Mrs J. Hutch

Mrs Hutch wrote this letter to

A ☐ ask for the principal's advice.

B ☐ explain how Sarah became ill.

C ☐ ask for a medical certificate.

D ☐ excuse her daughter from school.

2.
> **herman ze german**
> SAUSAGES
>
> HELLO FRIENDS,
>
> UNFORTUNATELY HERMAN STILL HAS A FEW THINGS THAT NEED TO BE FIXED AND THEREFORE HAS TO CLOSE THE SHOP THIS WEEKEND. ☹
>
> WE WILL BE BACK FOR YOU ON MONDAY.
>
> THANK YOU FOR YOUR UNDERSTANDING.
>
> XXX HERMAN

A ☐ Herman is looking for someone who can fix things.

B ☐ Herman has gone to see some friends.

C ☐ Herman will not open his shop this weekend.

D ☐ Herman needs to buy a few things this weekend.

3.

Because plastic isn't biodegradable, it's certain to outlive you by about a millennium or so. Each year thousands of marine animals choke to death on plastic trash they mistake for snacks. Our love for plastic disposables has also led to a flood of plastic trash the size of Texas in the North Pacific Ocean – not surprising when you consider that Americans run through about 100 billion plastic bags annually.

The best slogan for this text is:

A ☐ Don't eat endangered marine animals.
B ☐ Help keep Texas clean.
C ☐ Use less plastic.
D ☐ The North Pacific Ocean – a great place to go diving.

4.

PRET
Passionate About Food.

**My name is Luciano.
I'm the General Manager at this Pret Shop.**

My team and I meet every morning. We discuss the comments you've made, the good, the bad and the ugly. If we can deal with them ourselves, we will. If we can't, I'll forward this card to Julian Metcalf back at the office. I know he'll do what he can. If you have a minute, please do ask to speak to me or one of my team right now.

A ☐ In this shop customer feedback is welcome.
B ☐ This shop is only open in the morning.
C ☐ In this shop it only takes a minute to be served.
D ☐ In this shop you can get advice on how to improve your image.

5.

Victoria Coach Station 07 59

ATTENTION
Please wait inside until called
IT IS EXTREMELY DANGEROUS
to wait outside these gates.

The departure gate for your coach may be changed at late notice, you may also miss any messages on the screen.

T 21   21   Evan   09:00

A ☐ Passengers are asked to wait for their coach inside the building.
B ☐ The coach to Victoria leaves at 7.59.
C ☐ The messages on this screen will not be updated between 8.00 and 9.00.
D ☐ While waiting, passengers can watch videos on the screen.

Reading Part 2: Activities in Sydney

- These tourists (a–e) are looking for two activities to do in Sydney.
- First read the information about the tourists, then look at the activities (A–G) on the next page.
- In each case (a–e) find the **two** activities the tourists can do. Write the letters of the activities in the boxes next to the tourists' names.
- Some of the activities can be chosen more than once.

No.	Activity 1	Activity 2		The tourists
6/7				a) **Brodie and Jeanette Anstett** are in Sydney with their two children. Cindy (5) likes animals a lot and loves to get as close as possible to them. Their son Jamie is very fond of water so the Anstetts would like to get out of town for a little while.
8/9				b) **Priscilla Thornton** (31) is training to be a classical singer so she would be very interested in finding out what is going on behind the scenes of a musical theatre. After that she wouldn't mind having coffee in a nice neighbourhood and then do some shopping there.
10/11				c) **Paul and Tony** (25) It's their first holiday together. They are very interested in Australia's past – especially the beginnings and the time of the first prisoners. They would like to spend the afternoon at the sea in a relaxed and friendly environment.

12/13	d) **Clarisse Daniels** (70) would like to see some Australian animals but does not want to spend more than $ 20 on admission fees. She would also like to go to a part of Sydney where she can see both the old and the new face of the city.
14/15	e) **Taylor March** (20) is a very fit young man and would like to get a good view of Sydney in a special and exciting way. In the afternoon he would like to go to a museum but cannot really spend any more money.

A) **Bondi Shark Museum**

The Bondi Shark Museum features displays of sharks, marlin and all kinds of marine creatures. There is also an art gallery featuring Australian marine and indigenous paintings. One can experience the wonders of the planet's oceans in seven galleries as well as in a relaxation room with seating, videos, sounds of the ocean, murals, paintings, activities and games.

Opening times: 9.30 am – 6 pm Monday to Friday
10 am – 4 pm Saturday & Sunday
Entry fee: $ 8 Adults, $ 6 Concession and $ 4 Children under 12

B) **Sydney Harbour Bridge / The Bridge Climb**

Sydney Harbour Bridge – also affectionately known as the 'Coathanger' – is the world's largest steel arch bridge, and, in its beautiful harbour location, has become a renowned international symbol of Australia. The Bridge Climb is a 3 ½ hour guided journey to the top of the Sydney Harbour Bridge, 134 metres above Sydney Harbour.
In climb groups of up to 14 people, you'll be led by one of Bridge Climb's professional Climb Leaders on an adventure of the world's most recognisable bridge.
Admission: Adults $ 188 (night), $ 198 (day)

C) Opera House

The Sydney Opera House is considered by many to be one of the wonders of the modern world. Performances by various companies are being conducted all the time at the Opera House.

Choose from a one or two-hour tour that take in the extraordinary history, breathtaking architecture and the unseen workings of the Opera House and its daily life or take you behind the scenes to stand on stage.

a) The Guided Walking Tour (60 min): $ 35.00
b) Guided Backstage Tour (120 min): $ 150.00

D) Bondi Beach

The closest ocean beach to the centre of Sydney, Bondi has become synonymous with Sydney's beach lifestyle and is a symbol of tolerance, thus being also popular with the gay and lesbian community. It is fringed by parks and apartments that overlook the blue waters and the white sand.

Spanning the length of the beach, and across busy Campbell Parade, is a string of eateries, shops, hotels and tourist outlets, which bustle with activity most of the time.

Only a 30-minute drive from the centre of Sydney brings you to Bondi Beach.

E) The Australian National Maritime Museum

The Australian National Maritime Museum has thousands of exhibits depicting Australia's history – from ancient times when Aboriginal people trapped fish and traded with Asian neighbours, right up to the present. Visitors can see what life was like for the criminals who were sent to Australia on the convict ships; how Australia's first submarine fought bravely (and lost) in World War I; what people packed when they sailed to a new life on these shores; why surfboards have become shorter; and more. Admission free of charge.

Opening Hours: Daily 09:00 to 17:00
Daily 09:00 to 18:00 in January

F) The Rocks

The Rocks is the foundation place of Sydney and Australia, and is often described as "Sydney's outdoor museum".

The Rocks is the oldest area of Sydney and has recently undergone an amazing metamorphosis, the old district being transformed into a vibrant pocket of cafés and restaurants and interesting tourist shops and stalls. This has been achieved without destroying the area's Old World charm and historic buildings.

The Sydney Visitor Centre in The Rocks (open daily 9.30 am to 5.30 pm) is an excellent starting point.

G) Taronga Zoo

Taronga Zoo features Australia's finest collection of native animals and a diverse collection of exotic species. What makes Taronga something special is its location. It is situated on elevated land along the waterfront. The Taronga Zoo has its own jetty and you are able to step off the boat and walk directly into the zoo.

If you would like to get up close to the animals and have your picture taken, then try the *Animal Encounters* experience. For a small fee, with the assistance of the rangers, you can enter the enclosures of some of the animals on display and have your picture taken by a professional.

Opening Hours: Daily 09:00 to 17:00
Admission: Adults $ 41, Pensioners $ 28, Children (4–15) $ 20

Reading Part 3: HIP Berlin

- Read the text and the statements on the opposite page.
- Put a tick (✓) in the box next to the correct answer.
- Only one answer is correct in each case.

A cold wind is blowing through Mitte, the once dull, grey district in central Berlin, which is now becoming a popular place for creative people from all over the world. Davide Grazioli, who is used to warmer weather, pulls his black woolly hat over his head and walks up Kastanien Allee – now sometimes called Casting
5 Alley because of all the wannabe film directors and actors who come to its cafés. Grazioli is an Italian artist. Three years ago, he moved to Berlin from Milan with his wife and young daughter, and though his German is very basic, he enjoys the city. Berlin is "a place for new beginnings," Grazioli says. "Being in an unfinished place has a huge impact on you. In Milan I wouldn't have allowed myself
10 to do something new."

Germany has a lot of fine qualities, but being hip isn't usually thought to be one of them. Up-and-coming artists, especially ones from abroad, used to go to London, Amsterdam or New York City rather than Hamburg, Munich or Cologne. As for Berlin, it hasn't been on the international list of cool cities since the
15 early 1930s. If foreigners came to visit, they were hippies, spies, U.S. Presidents or peeping tourists, who wanted to look at communism from a safe distance. But two decades after the Wall that cut through Berlin's heart came tumbling down, the city is once again a happening place. It draws a large number of international designers, writers, architects, musicians and visual artists like Grazioli, some just
20 to visit, many to stay.

While the cost of housing can be a big problem in other cities, Berlin's many inexpensive places to live are making it even more attractive. A big number of cheap apartments and empty factories and warehouses in the formerly communist eastern half has brought prices down throughout the city. You can get studio
25 space for next to nothing. Even in Mitte, the center of Berlin's new *Szene*, newly renovated apartments rent for less than one quarter of what you'd pay in London. That's a big draw. But Berlin isn't just cheap. Some go there because it is not set in brick, stone and concrete, but in the process of redefining itself. A sort of artsy fashion, plus the underground music scene, plus 170 museums and many reno-
30 vated monuments have all helped to make tourism increase fast. The number of visitors from abroad is up 2.5 times since 2003. Just as dramatic is the flood of foreigners moving to Berlin to live – they now make up almost 1 in 7 of its 3.5 million inhabitants. The number of non-German Europeans living in Berlin has more than doubled since 2003. There are now more of them than Turks, who
35 long made up the largest group of foreigners. In Mitte, almost 30 % of the population comes from abroad; before the Wall came down, the only foreigners were a few East bloc diplomats. The new arrivals are making Berlin's population younger: unlike the Germans themselves, whose birthrate is among the lowest in

Europe, the foreigners are either bringing their children with them, or having them there. Mitte has the largest proportion of children under the age of 6. And that's not counting Brad Pitt and Angelina Jolie, who show up from time to time with their kids.

It's 2 p.m. on a Tuesday afternoon, and Davide Grazioli is sitting in a café with an Italian friend, Adalberto Andorlini, a producer who designs conferences. Tired of Milan, he and his family flew to Berlin and fell in love with it. "The kids didn't want to go back to Italy," Andorlini says. Life is very different from the stressful atmosphere he was once used to. "Here there's a community of people with a lot of free time to see one another," Andorlini says. "In Milan if you're not working at 8 p.m. you're not successful. I feel like I'm on holiday." The conversation turns to comparisons. "Berlin is like Paris in the '30s," Andorlini says. "It's a place where artists gather and things spring out of nothing." Grazioli isn't so sure. "It's more like New York in the '60s," he says. "All those abandoned lofts in SoHo."

It's an interesting discussion, without an obvious right answer. But the fact that it's even a topic of kaffeeklatsch in a trendy café on a Tuesday afternoon is just one more sign that Berlin is back.

Based on: Peter Gumbel: HIP, Time Magazine. November 16, 2009.

16. Mitte is a district in Berlin which
    A ☐ attracts people from different nations.
    B ☐ is famous for its hat shops.
    C ☐ has a street also known as Casting Alley.
    D ☐ both A + C

17. Davide Grazioli likes being in Berlin because
    A ☐ it is easy to become a film director here.
    B ☐ he can improve his German.
    C ☐ he enjoys the weather here.
    D ☐ he loves living in a city that is in the process of change.

18. Berlin attracted creative people
    A ☐ in the late 1930s.
    B ☐ between the early 1930s and the fall of the Wall.
    C ☐ two decades after the fall of the Wall.
    D ☐ both A + C

19. In terms of housing Berlin
    - A ☐ experiences rising rents.
    - B ☐ offers lots of cheap living space.
    - C ☐ has newly renovated apartments that are cheaper than in London.
    - D ☐ both B + C

20. Tourist numbers have
    - A ☐ doubled yearly since 2003.
    - B ☐ risen because of the many different things Berlin offers.
    - C ☐ risen because of the excellent underground system.
    - D ☐ gone up because of the many Germans who come to the city.

21. The foreigners living in Berlin
    - A ☐ make up 2.5 million people.
    - B ☐ are one seventh of the total population.
    - C ☐ have nearly doubled in numbers since 2003.
    - D ☐ make up half of the inhabitants of Mitte.

22. The population of Berlin is becoming younger because
    - A ☐ the birthrate among Germans is rising.
    - B ☐ children under 6 can get financial support from the state.
    - C ☐ lots of foreign families with children live in Berlin.
    - D ☐ both B + C

23. Adalberto Andorlini is
    - A ☐ meeting his friend in a café in Berlin.
    - B ☐ an Italian film producer.
    - C ☐ an Italian who has moved from Berlin back to Milan.
    - D ☐ on holiday in Berlin without his family.

24. The two Italians
    - A ☐ prefer Italian working hours to those in Berlin.
    - B ☐ think Berlin is a very hectic place.
    - C ☐ compare Berlin with Amsterdam.
    - D ☐ enjoy the lifestyle of Berlin.

25. The author's main intention is to inform the reader about
    - A ☐ the housing situation in Berlin.
    - B ☐ tourism in Berlin after the fall of the Wall.
    - C ☐ the history of Berlin.
    - D ☐ how Berlin is becoming attractive to other Europeans.

Reading: Candidate Answer Sheet   Name: _____

For students: Put a tick (✓) in the correct box.

Part 1

Number	A	B	C	D
1				
2				
3				
4				
5				

/ 5 P

Part 2 (Sydney)

Number	Name	A	B	C	D	E	F	G
6/7	a) Brodie and Jeanette							
8/9	b) Priscilla Thornton							
10/11	c) Paul and Tony							
12/13	d) Clarisse Daniels							
14/15	e) Taylor March							

/ 10 P

Part 3

Number	A	B	C	D
16				
17				
18				
19				
20				
21				
22				
23				
24				
25				

/ 10 P

/ 25 P

Writing Part 1: A Social Networking Site

You want to join a new social networking site.

- Complete the form below.
- You must fill in each item. You may use your imagination.
- Just use **keywords** *(Stichwörter),* do not write complete sentences.
- Remember: Correct spelling is important!

MyFACE – Registration Form

Thank you for choosing MyFACE. To register, please fill in the form below. Be careful about giving your real name.

(1) **Screen Name:** _____
    Age: _____
    Sex: _____ | 1 P |

(2) **What do you like most about yourself?** (name two aspects)
    - _____
    - _____ | 1 P |

(3) **What are you really good at?**
    _____ | 1 P |

(4) **What type of films do you like?**
    _____ | 1 P |

(5) **Why would you like to join MyFACE?**
    _____ | 1 P |

/5 P

Writing Part 2: Finding a Job

- Read what Ranjit has written.
- Then write back, answering all of his questions.
- You must write a minimum of 100 words. Do not use Internet slang.

E-pinion   Search the Web   ◯ go

E-pinion ▶ Community ▶ Public   User Name _____   ☐ Remember Me?
...... 🗁 jobs   Password _____   ◯ Log in.

| Register | Help | Members List | Calendar | Arcade | Articles | Today's Post | Journal ▽ | Search ▽ |

Name: Ranjit (15)
Joined E-pinion: January 2012
Location: Bradford

Hi guys,

I'll be finished with school next summer but I just don't know what to do afterwards. I'm interested in many things but I'm not sure what kind of job I want to do. Maybe you can help me. What are you planning to do? Is making a lot of money more important for you than doing a job you really enjoy?
I'm not sure where to get help on how to decide about my future.
Any ideas?
Will life be very different after school ... what do you think?

Please write soon.
Ranjit

Hi Ranjit,

___

Inhalt: ____ / 5 P   Sprache: ____ / 5 P   Gesamt: ____ / 10 P

2012-17

Writing Part 3: Two Tickets

Linie 1

Eines der erfolgreichsten deutschen Musicals!

Schon über 1 000 Aufführungen in Berlin!

Eine junge Ausreißerin vom Land kommt am Bahnhof Zoo an. Sie ist auf der Suche nach ihrem „Märchenprinzen", einem Berliner Rockmusiker. Ihre Suche führt sie mit der U-Bahn-Linie 1 durch ganz verschiedene Bezirke Berlins, und sie begegnet vielen unterschiedlichen Typen, die von ihren ganz persönlichen Schicksalen erzählen.

Eine Show, ein Drama, ein Musical über das Leben und Überleben in der Großstadt, zum Lachen und Weinen, zum Träumen – und zum Nachdenken über sich selbst.

Arena Tour!

Erleben Sie die modernste Multifunktionsarena Europas aus Perspektiven, die den Zuschauern sonst verborgen bleiben. Bei unseren Besucherführungen erfahren Sie alles, was Sie schon immer über die O_2 World wissen wollten, z. B. „Wo bleibt das Eis bei Konzertveranstaltungen?". Unsere Guides lassen keine Frage unbeantwortet.

Die 60-minütige Tour führt Sie vom Eingangsbereich über die Premium Bereiche und die Suiten bis hin zu den Backstage-Bereichen und dem Innenraum der Arena. Die geschulten Guides erklären Ihnen die architektonischen und technischen Besonderheiten der O_2 World und geben Ihnen Einblicke in die Abläufe bei Konzert- und Sportveranstaltungen.

Ein Highlight für alle Sport-Fans ist der Besuch der Mannschaftskabine des wiederholten Deutschen Meisters Eisbären Berlin.

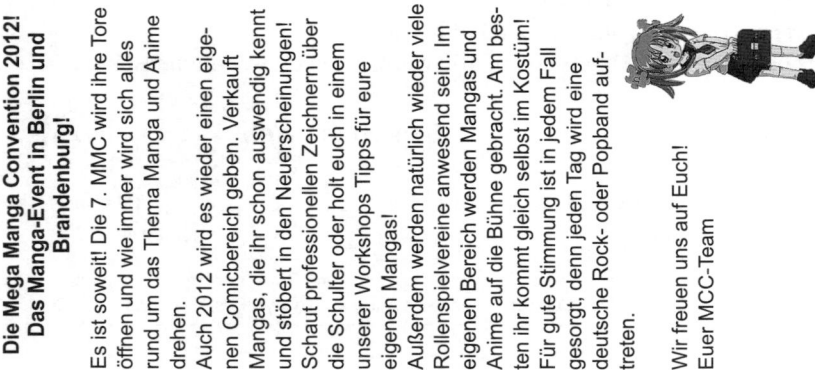

Die Mega Manga Convention 2012!
Das Manga-Event in Berlin und Brandenburg!

Es ist soweit! Die 7. MMC wird ihre Tore öffnen und wie immer wird sich alles rund um das Thema Manga und Anime drehen.

Auch 2012 wird es wieder einen eigenen Comicbereich geben. Verkauft Mangas, die ihr schon auswendig kennt und stöbert in den Neuerscheinungen! Schaut professionellen Zeichnern über die Schulter oder holt euch in einem unserer Workshops Tipps für eure eigenen Mangas!

Außerdem werden natürlich wieder viele Rollenspielvereine anwesend sein. Im eigenen Bereich werden Mangas und Anime auf die Bühne gebracht. Am besten ihr kommt gleich selbst im Kostüm! Für gute Stimmung ist in jedem Fall gesorgt, denn jeden Tag wird eine deutsche Rock- oder Popband auftreten.

Wir freuen uns auf Euch!
Euer MCC-Team

Writing Part 3: Two Tickets

As a present for your birthday your parents want to give you two tickets for an event. You would like to go there with your Irish friend who is coming to visit you for a week.
- Read the three texts about the events/activities you can choose from.
- Choose **two** events/activities.
- Write an e-mail to your friend telling him/her about the two events/activities you have chosen.
- For each one of them say what kind of event/activity it is and mention at least two more aspects that are important.
- **Do not translate word for word**, just give the main information used in these texts.
- Write complete sentences and use correct English.

To: _____@hotmail.com

Ref: Let's go out

Hey _____,

I've just got a super birthday present – two tickets for an event of my choice. And that's something that we could do together when you are here. Here are the two events I find most interesting.

_____
_____
_____
_____

Which of the two would you like to go to? Tell me what you think.
☺ _____

Inhalt: /6 P   Sprache: /4 P   Gesamt: /10 P

Lösungsvorschläge

Listening Part 1: Conversations

Conversation 1

1 CUSTOMER: I bought these jeans here last week. I'm afraid I have to return them.
  ASSISTANT: Is there something wrong with them?
  CUSTOMER: No, nothing's wrong with them. It's just – they don't look right.
  ASSISTANT: Well if they don't fit properly, I am sure we can fix that.
5 CUSTOMER: Don't get me wrong – they fit perfectly. But I wore them to a party and my boyfriend didn't like them much.
  ASSISTANT: I'm sorry, once you've worn them, you can't return them.

1. D
   Hinweis: "I bought these jeans here last week. I'm afraid I have to return them." (Z. 1), "No, nothing's wrong with them." (Z. 3)
   Bild B kann nicht zutreffend sein, da die Jeans in Bild B zerrissen ist. Zudem spricht die Person von ihrem Freund (Z. 6), was auch beweist, dass Bild D zutreffend sein muss.

Conversation 2

1 CUSTOMER 1: Did you see that? I can't believe it.
  CUSTOMER 2: Did I see what?
  CUSTOMER 1: Do you see the guy in the torn jeans … over there near the lift?
  CUSTOMER 2: The one in the green shirt? What about him?
5 CUSTOMER 1: I'm sure he has just let a CD slip into his bag.
  CUSTOMER 2: Really? That would be shoplifting. Do you think we should report it to one of the shop assistants?

2. E
   Hinweis: "Do you see the guy in the torn jeans … over there near the lift?" (Z. 3), "I'm sure he has just let a CD slip into his bag." (Z. 5)

Conversation 3

1 CUSTOMER 1: The food halls are on the seventh floor. Let's take the express elevator, it's right over there.
  CUSTOMER 2: Hm, sorry, I'd rather not take the elevator. The last time I did, it got stuck between two floors and I had to spend nearly 30 minutes in there
5   before someone managed to get us out. I almost panicked – you know how claustrophobic I can get.

CUSTOMER 1: Ouch, that sounds nasty. So let's take the escalator instead.
CUSTOMER 2: Okay ...

3. C

Hinweis: "Let's take the express elevator ..." (Z. 1/2), "So let's take the escalator instead." (Z. 7)
In Bild C zeigt jemand auf die Rolltreppe. Das passt genau zu dem, was im Dialog gesagt wird.

Conversation 4

CUSTOMER 1: Have you got another 10 minutes to spare? I saw this great pair of jeans the other day. I'd like to know what you think of them.
CUSTOMER 2: Oh, sure. Where did you see them?
CUSTOMER 1: Just around the corner – at "The Wild Bunch". It'll only take a few minutes.
CUSTOMER 2: "The Wild Bunch"? They're closed this week ... they're renovating.
CUSTOMER 1: Too bad, aww that's probably why the jeans were 20 % off.
CUSTOMER 2: Could be, but I bet they'll have great re-opening offers next week, too.

4. A

Hinweis: "The Wild Bunch" (Z. 4), "They're closed this week ... they're renovating." (Z. 6/7), "... they'll have great re-opening offers next week, too." (Z. 9/10)

Listening Part 2: Radio Ads

Ad 1: Scary Maths

There's some disturbing maths coming out of Mississippi schools. Every hour about 1.5 Mississippi kids drop out. Added up, that's about 36 kids every day, over a thousand a month, that's nearly 13,000 kids every year. And that's where the math really gets scary, because kids who drop out are twice as likely to end up on drugs; almost three times more likely to end up unemployed or on welfare; and ten times more likely to go to jail. That costs Mississippi more than 458 million dollars every year. But as disturbing as the numbers are, it's not about numbers, it's about lives.

That's why we've launched "On the Bus", a program designed to keep Mississippi kids in school. So get on the bus. Log on to "onthebus.ms" and see how you can help. Because if you can help subtract just one number from the drop-out rate, well that's one life changed forever.

A message from State Farm Insurance and the Mississippi Department of Education.

http://www.onthebus.ms/ [12. 3. 2011]

5. A

> ✏ *Hinweis:* "Every hour about 1.5 Mississippi kids drop out." (Z. 1/2), "That's why we've launched 'On the Bus', a program designed to keep Mississippi kids in school." (Z. 9/10)

Ad 2: SA rhythm

1 Hey there, South Africa, I want you to grab your pen, your pencils, your drumsticks, hoot your hula, tap on your desk, bang your foot, whatever you do, just get ready to play the rhythm that shows our country is alive with possibility. It's a simple rhythm in two parts. So, listen up – this is how the first part goes.
5 *(music)*
And this is the second part. *(music)*
And that's it. Comes pretty naturally, doesn't it?
So, whoever you are and wherever you are, be a part of the rhythm of this nation. Right, now let's put it all together. *(music)*

http://www.brandsouthafrica.com/index.php/componenUcontenUarticle/21-static/39-radio-ads.html [12. 3. 2011]

6. C

> ✏ *Hinweis:* "... be a part of the rhythm of this nation" (Z. 8)

Ad 3: Identity Theft

1 *(music)*
MCGRUFF: When crime prevention is your life, your days don't stay quiet for long. *(telephone ringing)* What did I tell you? My name – McGruff, the crime dog. I wear a trench coat.
5 WOMAN *(on phone)*: McGruff – I need help!
MCGRUFF: That was a concerned citizen – and boy, did she sound concerned.
WOMAN: I'm very concerned.
MCGRUFF: What did I tell you?
WOMAN: Somebody took out a loan in my name. They are pretending to be me
10 and spending my money. I cannot ...
MCGRUFF: It's called identity theft and it's growing fast. Safeguard your personal information like your social security, credit card or bank account num-

bers – on the phone, online, even around the house because half of identity theft occurs by someone you think you know.
15 Learn more from the National Crime Prevention Council at NCPC.org. Take it from McGruff: Keep your identity to yourself and take a bite out of crime. A message from this station, the US Department of Justice, Crime Prevention, Coalition of America and the National Crime Prevention Council.

http://www.ncpc.org/topics/neighborhood-watch [12. 10. 2011)

7. A
   ✒ *Hinweis: "Safeguard your personal information ..." (Z. 11/12)*

Ad 4: Safer London

1 You are someone who lives in London, someone who takes the tube, gets the bus, hails a cab, you're someone who stands on the right, holds open doors, smiles at strangers. You are someone with a partner, friends and family, mates and colleagues. You are someone with hopes and fears, ambitions and dreams, a
5 past and a future. And you are someone who knows that terrorists won't succeed, as long as someone calls the police to report anything suspicious. You are that someone. If you see anything suspicious, a bag, a vehicle or just the way a person's behaving, don't leave it to someone else. If you suspect it, report it. Call 999, Metropolitan Police. Working together for a safer London.

http://content.met.police.uk/ [12. 10. 2011]

8. C
   ✒ *Hinweis: "If you see anything suspicious, ... report it." (Z. 7/8)*

Listening Part 3: Ellis Island

1 *(introductory music)*
GUIDE'S VOICE: Good morning everybody and welcome to Ellis Island Immigration Museum here in New York Harbor. In front of you is the statue of Annie Moore, a 15-year-old girl from Ireland, who was the very first immi-
5 grant to set foot on this island when it opened as an immigration center in 1892.
When the center was closed in 1954, more than 12 million people had come to America through this port. To most, Ellis Island had been an Isle of Hope, a stopping point on the way to a better life – as it had been for Annie Moore.
10 Please press button A to listen to her story.

ANNIE'S VOICE: My name is Annie Moore and I was born in Ireland in 1877. My moment of glory I had on the first of January 1892 when I was the first person to set foot on Ellis Island.

We had set off from Cobh (*say:* Cove), Co. Cork, Ireland 12 days before. Oh, I remember that journey so well. I felt both excited and sad at the same time. Excited to see my parents and older siblings, who had left Ireland two years earlier in order to find work in America. You see, people couldn't get jobs in Ireland in those days and there were political problems with the British. America was the only hope.

My family's hopes had been fulfilled. They had found jobs, a place to live and they had enough money for food and clothing. Life was better than it had been in Ireland. But I also felt so sad about leaving my home, my friends, my relatives in Ireland.

I wondered if I would ever see them again. There were so many questions in my mind. What were the American people like? Would I find friends there? Were the streets really paved with gold? Did they eat Irish stew in America?

I remember the ship journey so well. I stood in line with my two younger brothers, Philip and Anthony. We were steerage passengers on the steamship Nevada. For us the conditions were miserable, with so many people crowded into a tiny, dark, foul-smelling space below deck. The whole journey was a nightmare. There weren't enough toilets or washrooms, it was freezing cold and people were constantly getting seasick.

I had to watch my brothers very closely to make sure they were safe. But at least I knew that they were healthy. This was important because there was going to be a medical inspection on arrival in New York. There we would be examined for symptoms of diphtheria, tuberculosis, typhoid and other weird diseases I couldn't even pronounce.

Anyway, to pass the time we played cards, sang, danced and talked. All around me I could hear Germans and Italians practicing their English. And most important of all were the rehearsals for answering the immigration inspectors' questions:

(STERN MALE VOICE:)

By whom was passage paid? Have you ever been in prison? Are you an anarchist? Are you a polygamist?

ANNIE'S VOICE: On the first of January 1892 the ship reached New York. The Statue of Liberty welcomed us as we sailed into the harbor. The greatness of Ms Liberty overcame us. Nobody said a word for she was like a goddess and we knew she symbolized the powerful country which was to be our future home. And then ... we saw Ellis Island ... and everyone started to cheer and cry.

Suddenly I heard someone shout "Ladies first" ... and I remember being pushed ahead of a muscular German man by my brothers. Then I realized I was the first one off the ship! I was very surprised when an official gave me a $ 10 gold piece. I had never seen so much money before in my whole life, and I did not know why he had given it to me. Was it because of my 15th birthday? Then he explained that Ellis Island was new, and the $ 10 was a present to the first person to set foot on the newly-opened Ellis Island immigration port.

GUIDE'S VOICE: Now, over 100 years later, a statue of Annie and her brothers stands on Ellis Island. A similar statue can be found in Cobh (*say:* Cove), Ireland, where they began their voyage. There is even a song about Annie's story. Press button B if you want *to listen to it.*

ased on: www.mayolibrary.ie/.../LifeStories/AnnieMoore/
http://www.ellisisland.org/Eiinfo/press_AnnieMoore.asp
http://www.coedu.usf.edu/culture/Story/Story_Ireland.htm
http://www.rootstelevision.com/blogs/megans-rootsworld/2007/12/a_pair_of_ellis_island_videos.html
[12. 2. 2011]

9. Yes
  ◢ **Hinweis:** "It opened as an immigration center in 1892" (Z. 5/6), "... was closed in 1954" (Z. 7)

10. No
  ◢ **Hinweis:** "We had set off from Cobh, Co. Cork, Ireland 12 days before." (Z. 14)

11. Yes
  ◢ **Hinweis:** "Excited to see my parents ..., who had left Ireland two years earlier ..." (Z. 16/17)

12. Yes
  ◢ **Hinweis:** "What were the American people like? Would I find friends there? Were the streets really paved with gold?" (Z. 25/26)

13. No
  ◢ **Hinweis:** "For us the conditions were miserable ..." (Z. 29), "The whole journey was a nightmare." (Z. 30/31)

14. No
  ◢ **Hinweis:** "But at least I knew that they were healthy."(Z. 33/34)

15. Yes
  ◢ **Hinweis:** "And most important of all were the rehearsals for answering the immigration inspectors' questions" (Z. 39–41)

16. Yes
    Hinweis: "The greatness of Ms Liberty overcame us. Nobody said a word ..." (Z. 46/47)

17. No
    Hinweis: "... was a present to the first person to set foot on the newly-opened Ellis Island immigration port." (Z. 56–58)

18. No
    Hinweis: "Life was better than it had been in Ireland." (Z. 21/22)
    Auch wenn die Reise hart war, so war die Auswanderung dennoch die Verwirklichung eines Wunsches. ("My family's hopes had been fulfilled." Z. 20)

Listening Part 4: CouchSurfing

VINCENT: This is Vincent Canary from *TTR Radio,* and welcome to our weekly edition of *"Have Your Say"!* Ever heard about a thing called "CouchSurfing"? You think it's a way to get rid of old furniture? *(chuckle)* Far from it! CouchSurfing is all about ... travelling. And today you have the chance to find out more from my guests here in the studio.

First let me introduce Dido Bransted, who has just turned 18 and wants to spend her summer holidays surfing Europe's couches.

DIDO: Hi.

VINCENT: Also here with us is her mother Linda, who will tell us why she is not too fond of the idea. Welcome, Linda.

LINDA: Good afternoon.

VINCENT: And last but not least, we have Jonathan Wilder, who travelled the world for a year after finishing school.

Jonathan, you've written about your various CouchSurfing experiences in a blog. Would you tell our listeners something about CouchSurfing in general, just to give them an idea ...?

JONATHAN: Sure. You know, it's only because of CouchSurfing that I was able to stay abroad for such a long time. This experience really changed the way I see the world.

But let me give you an idea of what CouchSurfing is all about: Let's say you want to go to Amsterdam for 4 days. First you go to the CouchSurfing-website and look for people from Amsterdam who have a "couch" on offer, which most often means a bed in their home. You explain what you are interested in doing while you're there and then you get several offers for places to stay. After choosing one of them, you contact your host, agree on the details of your travel plans and ... off you go to Amsterdam to meet new people who know the city really well!

LINDA: But that's just the point, Jonathan. You have no idea who these people are you'll be staying with! I don't even want to think of what could happen to Dido ...!

DIDO: Oh come on, Mum, I'm already 18 and I know what I'm doing ...

LINDA: ... but that doesn't make it any less dangerous, Darling! You see, there are people out there who could do all sorts of ...

JONATHAN: ... Hold on. I understand your worries, Mrs Bransted. But the CouchSurfing program has a system of safety features. It sort of works like a neighbourhood watch program. For example, the good and bad experiences people have had are published on the Internet, and if anything terrible has happened, these people are taken off the list. But – as always – there is no absolute guarantee. By the way, these safety features are there to protect both sides of the deal, hosts and guests.

DIDO: See Mum, there's no need to worry. They're probably people just like us ...

LINDA: And would we have to let a stranger stay at our place, too?

JONATHAN: You don't have to, Mrs Bransted. If you don't want to have somebody sleeping on your couch, you don't have to pay the hosts. Instead there are other ways Dido can show that she's thankful for her host's hospitality, like cooking a nice meal ...

DIDO: That's the whole idea, money's not important here. CouchSurfing is a really cheap way of travelling. I'll only need money for the trip itself, for food, bus tickets, stuff like that. Cool, eh!

LINDA: Don't tell me there are people out there who don't expect to be paid ... one way or another ...

DIDO: Oh Mum, you're being so negative! The people who make such an offer have a vision. They want to connect people, help make the world a better place.

JONATHAN: You're right there, Dido. The first CouchSurfer, who later founded the organisation, was a student who didn't want to travel like Mr Tourist anymore. You know, in and out of hotels, visiting postcard sights but never really getting to know the people and their culture. And there is a clear mission: Only when you experience a culture from within can real understanding and intercultural tolerance develop. And isn't this what a globalised world really needs?

LINDA: I do see your point there, Jonathan, and the idea of meeting people from all over the world when you're young and don't have much money sounds fascinating. But still – a girl travelling on her own ...

VINCENT: I see. You don't want to spend the summer holidays worrying about her, is that right? Well, Dido, your Mum would probably feel better if you didn't travel by yourself.
DIDO: I wasn't planning to in the first place. It's much more fun to travel with a friend. Fiona wants to come along.
LINDA: Fiona? Aha, two girls! As if that makes a difference! ...
VINCENT: *(interrupting them)* I think this is a perfect time for a break. We'll be back in a minute with Jonathan, who will be telling us some fascinating stories of his CouchSurfing travels across the world ... *(fading out)*

Based on: http://www.couchsurfing.org/about.html/faq [22. 11. 2009]

19. A
 Hinweis: "CouchSurfing is all about ... travelling." (Z. 4)

20. C
 Hinweis: "This experience really changed the way I see the world." (Z. 18/19)

21. A
 Hinweis: "First you go to the CouchSurfing-website and look for people ... who have a 'couch' on offer, which most often means a bed in their home." (Z. 21–23)

22. B
 Hinweis: "It sort of works like a neighbourhood watch program. For example, the good and bad experiences people have had are published on the Internet ..." (Z. 35–37)

23. C
 Hinweis: "...you don't have to pay the hosts." (Z. 45)

24. B
 Hinweis: "Only when you experience a culture from within can real understanding and intercultural tolerance develop." (Z. 60/61)

25. B
 Hinweis: "But still – a girl travelling on her own ..." (Z. 65), "Fiona? Aha, two girls! As if that makes a difference! ..." (Z. 71)

Reading Part 1: Short Texts

1. D
   Hinweis: "My daughter ... has taken ill", "enclosing a medical certificate from the attending doctor"
2. C
   Hinweis: "Herman ... has to close the shop this weekend."
3. C
   Hinweis: "plastic isn't biodegradable", "thousands of marine animals choke to death on plastic trash"
4. A
   Hinweis: "We discuss the comments you've made ..."
5. A
   Hinweis: "ATTENTION! Please wait inside ..."

Reading Part 2: Activities in Sydney

6./7.   D, G
   Hinweis: Character: "Their son Jamie is very fond of water ..."
   → Activity D: "ocean beach"
   Character: "Cindy (5) likes animals a lot ..."
   → Activity G: "Taronga Zoo"
8./9.   C, F
   Hinweis: Character: "Priscilla ... would be very interested in finding out what is going on behind the scenes of a musical theatre."
   → Activity C: "Choose from a one or two-hour tour that ...take you behind the scenes"
   Character: "... she wouldn't mind having coffee in a nice neighbourhood and then do some shopping there."
   → Activity F: "cafés and restaurants and interesting tourist shops and stalls"
10./11.   D, E
   Hinweis: Character: "They would like to spend the afternoon at the sea in a relaxed and friendly environment."
   → Activity D: "ocean beach", "Bondi ... is a symbol of tolerance, thus being also popular with the gay and lesbian community"
   Character: "They are very interested in Australia's past."

→ Activity E: *"The Australian National Maritime Museum has thousands of exhibits depicting Australia's history."*

12./13. A, F

Hinweis: Character: *"Clarisse Daniels (70) would like to see some Australian animals but does not want to spend more than $20 in admission fees."*
→ Activity A: *"The Bondi Shark Museum features displays of sharks, marlin and all kinds of marine creatures.", "Entry fee: $8 Adults"*
Character: *"She would also like ... to see both the old and the new face of the city."*
→ Activity F: *"The Rocks is the oldest area of Sydney and has recently undergone an amazing metamorphosis."*

14./15. B, E

Hinweis: Character: *"Taylor March (20) is a very fit young man and would like to get a good view of Sydney in a special and exciting way"*
→ Activity B: *"The Bridge Climb is a 3 ½ hour guided journey to the top of Sydney Harbour Bridge, 134 metres above Sydney Harbour."*
Character: *"... would like to go to a museum but cannot really spend any more money."*
→ Activity E: *"The Australian National Maritime Museum", "Admission free of charge"*

Reading Part 3: HIP Berlin

16. D

Hinweis: *"... is now becoming a popular place for creative people from all over the world." (Z. 2/3), "Kastanien Allee – now sometimes called Casting Alley" (Z. 4/5)*

17. D

Hinweis: *"... a place for new beginnings" (Z. 8), "Being in an unfinished place has a huge impact on you." (Z. 8/9)*

18. C

Hinweis: *"But two decades after the Wall ... came tumbling down, the city is once again a happening place. It draws a large number of international designers, writers, architects, musicians and visual artists ... many to stay." (Z. 16–20)*

19. D

    ✏ *Hinweis:* "Berlin's many inexpensive places to live are making it even more attractive."(Z. 21–22), "… newly renovated apartments rent for less than one quarter of what you'd pay in London." (Z. 25–26)

20. B

    ✏ *Hinweis:* "A sort of artsy fashion, plus the underground music scene, plus 170 museums and many renovated monuments have all helped to make tourism increase fast." (Z. 28–30)

21. B

    ✏ *Hinweis:* "… foreigners moving to Berlin to live – they now almost make up 1 in 7" (Z. 32)

22. C

    ✏ *Hinweis:* "… foreigners are either bringing their children with them, or having them there." (Z. 39/40)

23. A

    ✏ *Hinweis:* "… is sitting in a cafe with an Italian friend." (Z. 43/44)

24. D

    ✏ *Hinweis:* "… very different from the stressful atmosphere he was once used to." (Z. 46/47), "I feel like I'm on holiday." (Z. 49)

25. D

    ✏ *Hinweis:* "The number of non-German Europeans living in Berlin has more than doubled …" (Z. 33/34)

Writing Part 1: A Social Networking Site

✏ *Hinweis:* Alle Eintragungen müssen sprachlich korrekt sein. Es sollen nur Stichwörter eingetragen werden. Ein Punkt wird aber nur gegeben, wenn diese Wörter richtig geschrieben sind. Bei der folgenden Beispiellösung werden verschiedene Alternativen gegeben.

1. *Screen Name:* Monster
   Age: 16/17
   Sex: male/female

2. My sense of humour / I'm quite courageous. / I'm very friendly. / I like to help others. / I'm understanding. / I'm open-minded.

3. painting / playing guitar / playing football / math

4. science fiction / comedy / action / thrillers
5. to make new friends / to see what other people are doing / to show my favorite pictures / to arrange get-togethers with my friends

Writing Part 2: Finding a Job

Hinweis: Bei der Beantwortung einer E-Mail ist es wichtig, dass alle gestellten Fragen beantwortet werden. Der Text klingt flüssiger, wenn typische Redewendungen verwendet werden.

Hi Ranjit,
I'm not sure either what I'm going to do after leaving school in June. I was thinking of studying engineering but I'm afraid it will be too difficult. Ideally, I would like to have both, a decent salary and a job that I enjoy. I think earning a lot of money is not that important, but there are some jobs that only pay a minimum wage, so I would steer clear of those. That's why I might study engineering or architecture. It's fascinating and I'll probably earn a reasonable salary later on. If you are not sure what to do, you could talk to a student counselor at your school and to your parents.
Of course, life will be different after school, especially if you move out of your parents' house or leave your home city, everything will change.
I'm looking forward to hearing about your decision.
Best,
(your name)

Writing Part 3: Two Tickets

Hinweis: Bei dieser Mediationsaufgabe müssen nur zwei der drei Aktivitäten beschrieben werden. Die Texte sollen nicht übersetzt werden, sondern es soll in eigenen Worten erklärt werden, worum es geht, und es sollen jeweils zwei weitere Punkte genannt werden. Im Lösungsbeispiel werden alle drei Aktivitäten präsentiert. Du solltest dir in der Prüfung die beiden Aktivitäten aussuchen, über die du am besten schreiben kannst.

Hey John,
I've just got a super birthday present – two tickets for an event of my choice. And that's something that we could do together when you are here. Here are the two events I find most interesting.

One option is a musical theatre performance called Linie 1. It's about a girl who runs away from home and goes to Berlin, looking for her prince charming, a Berlin rock musician. On the way along the "U-Bahn Linie 1", she meets different people who each tell her their personal story.

Another activity we could do together is the Arena tour. This is a 60-minute guided tour that leads you through the different areas of the huge O_2 World. We can go backstage and see the changing rooms of the famous ice hockey team, the "Eisbären Berlin". The building itself is also supposed to be very fascinating because of its impressive architecture.

We could also go to the Mega Manga Convention in Berlin together. You can sell used Mangas there, and watch the professional Manga illustrators at work. We could take part in a workshop and learn how to make mangas ourselves. There will be role play clubs present as well and every day there will be a performance by a German rock or pop band.

Which of the two would you like to go to? Tell me what you think.

Best,

(your name)

Bildnachweis:

S. 2012-2: Radio © PRILL Mediendesign – fotolia.de
S. 2012-3: Annie © amerune, lizenziert unter cc-by-2.0
S. 2012-9: Sydney Harbour Bridge: © Showface / Dreamstime.com
S. 2012-10: Opera House: © Dan Breckwoldt / Dreamstime.com, Bondi Beach © http://www.sydney-travelguide.net/wp-content/uploads/bondi-beach.jpg, The Australian National Maritime Museum: © http://www.sydneyontheweb.com/images/photos/australian_national_maritime_museum.jpg
S. 2012-11: The Rocks: © http://www.familyadventuretravelworks.com/wpcontent/uploads/2011/04/Austrsyd_the_rocks_sydney.jpg, Taronga Zoo: © http://www.sydney.com.au/images/zoo-lions.jpg
S. 2012-16: Social network: © http://www.worldwidehippies.com/2012/05/22/my-screened-and-unscreened-friends/
S. 2012-18: Arena: © DerRobert, lizenziert unter cc-by-2.0 , Linie 1: © ullstein bild - Günter Schneider, Manga Convention: © http://comic-culture-verlag.de/wb/media/Bilder%20in%20News/bunny-cosplay-bunny-tsukino.jpg

**Schriftliche Prüfung zum Mittleren Schulabschluss in Berlin
Englisch 2013**

Listening Part 1: Voicemail Messages

- You are going to hear two voicemail messages.
- You will hear the recording twice.
- There are four questions in this part, two questions for each message.
- Look at the pictures and then listen to the recording.
- Choose the correct picture and put a tick (✓) in the right box.

Message One

1. What time are the friends going to meet?

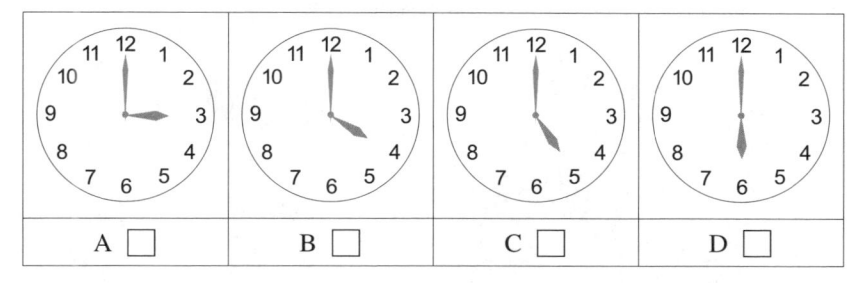

   A ☐   B ☐   C ☐   D ☐

2. What should Emily bring?

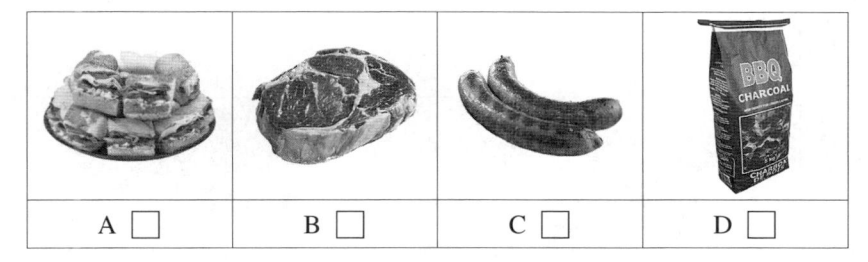

   A ☐   B ☐   C ☐   D ☐

Message Two

3. What is the new time table for the following day?

School: TUESDAY	School: TUESDAY	School: TUESDAY	School: TUESDAY
Math	Geography	Geography	Chemistry
Math	Chemistry	Chemistry	Geography
Chemistry	Art	Math	Art
Art	Art	Art	Art
A ☐	B ☐	C ☐	D ☐

4. Which of these teachers does Sam really like?

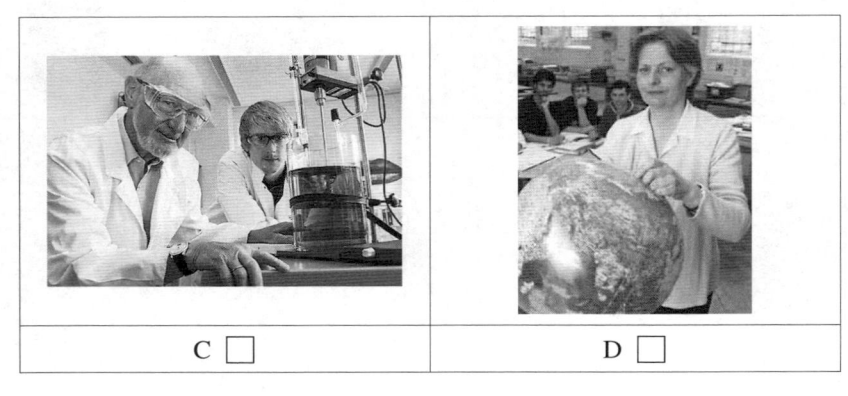

A ☐	B ☐
C ☐	D ☐

Listening Part 2: Radio Ads

Please note: You do not need to understand every word to do this task.

- You are going to listen to four radio ads (ads 1 to 4).
- You will hear the recording twice.
- Read the statements below first, then listen to the recording.
- For each ad choose the correct statement (A–C) and put a tick (✓) in the right box.
- There is only one correct statement for each ad.

5. **(Ad 1)**
   This recording is …
   A ☐ a warning against the dangers of diving.
   B ☐ an advertisement for diving lessons.
   C ☐ a report about a diver's experience.

6. **(Ad 2)**
   The Nebraska Bookstore …
   A ☐ has special opening hours for students.
   B ☐ specializes in books about animals.
   C ☐ offers the best price for used books.

7. **(Ad 3)**
   This ad invites you to …
   A ☐ come to the young scientists' exposition at the university.
   B ☐ visit the newly opened science fiction book shop.
   C ☐ spend time with your friends at the fun park.

8. **(Ad 4)**
   This radio ad informs you about …
   A ☐ a medical course at a university.
   B ☐ a new medication against insect bites.
   C ☐ how to protect yourself and others from getting the flu.

Listening Part 3: The Globe Theatre

- You are going to hear an audio tour.
- You will hear the recording twice.
- Read the ten statements below first, then listen to the recording.
- If you think a statement is correct, put a tick (✓) in the box for **YES**.
- If you think a statement is not correct, put a tick (✓) in the box for **NO**.

		Yes	No
9.	People loved going to the theatre in Shakespeare's days.	☐	☐
10.	The first performance at the new Globe Theatre took place in 1989.	☐	☐
11.	In some parts of the old Globe, people had to stand.	☐	☐
12.	On hot summer days there was a terrible smell in the cheap part of the theatre.	☐	☐
13.	Eating and drinking were not allowed during the play.	☐	☐
14.	In Shakespeare's time, the audience showed immediate and strong reactions to what they saw on stage.	☐	☐
15.	Molly became excited because she thought what she saw on stage was real.	☐	☐
16.	In Shakespeare's time, all of the roles were played by male actors.	☐	☐
17.	The actor Henry Condell found it difficult to act for the groundlings.	☐	☐
18.	The theatre had to pay Shakespeare some money for each performance of his plays.	☐	☐

Listening Part 4: Extreme Sports

- You are going to hear a talk show about extreme sports.
- There are four people in the talk show: Alison Freeman (the presenter), Greg Moore, Adam Sweeney and Marietta Collins.
- You will hear the recording twice.
- Read the statements below first, then listen to the recording.

- Put a tick (✓) in the box next to the correct statement.
- Only one statement is correct in each case.

19. The term BASE refers to
    A ☐ a bridge in New York used by BASE jumpers.
    B ☐ different objects and places you can jump from.
    C ☐ a parachute brand used for jumping.

20. BASE jumpers love
    A ☐ floating in the air as long as possible.
    B ☐ being under time pressure.
    C ☐ both A + B

21. A reason for Greg to do BASE jumping is
    A ☐ to become fit.
    B ☐ to do something illegal.
    C ☐ to test his limits.

22. The fight-or-flight response
    A ☐ is caused by adrenaline.
    B ☐ causes an unpleasant feeling when jumping.
    C ☐ both A + B

23. Adam joined the Search and Rescue Team because he
    A ☐ can deal with stress very well.
    B ☐ likes to help others and stay fit.
    C ☐ both A + B

24. Adam thinks that BASE jumpers
    A ☐ are a danger for other people.
    B ☐ should not be helped.
    C ☐ should use protective clothing.

25. According to Marietta, both Adam and Greg
    A ☐ endanger their lives but for different reasons.
    B ☐ are examples of modern day heroes.
    C ☐ both A + B

Listening: Candidate Answer Sheet   Name: _____

For students: Put a tick (✓) in the correct box.

Part 1

Number	A	B	C	D
1				
2				
3				
4				

/ 4 P

Part 2

Number	Ads	A	B	C
5	Ad 1			
6	Ad 2			
7	Ad 3			
8	Ad 4			

/ 4 P

Part 3

Number	Yes	No
9		
10		
11		
12		
13		
14		
15		
16		
17		
18		

/ 10 P

Part 4

Number	A	B	C
19			
20			
21			
22			
23			
24			
25			

/ 7 P

/ 25 P

Reading Part 1: Short Texts

- Look at the text and the statements in each task.
- What does the text say?
- Put a tick (✓) next to the statement that matches the text – **A**, **B**, **C** or **D**.
- There is only **one** correct statement for each sign.

1. I am a hairstylist from Beverly Hills. I have extensive experience as an educator for two of the top hair companies in the world. This Saturday I will be doing a cutting demonstration at a new up and coming salon in the city. I am going to be the Master Stylist there and need to show my skills. I need three models who need to be open to something modern and edgy …

   1. willing to change from long-mid length to a shorter bob type length
   2. curly haired (since cutting curly hair is a passion of mine)
   3. creative, funky, fun!!

   If interested please send a current picture with a clear view of your hair.

   Garreth

   P.S. my haircuts are $ 120 normally but free this time only!

   Garreth
   A ☐ charges haircut models $ 120.
   B ☐ is looking for haircut models.
   C ☐ is a haircut model.
   D ☐ is looking for three new assistants.

2. **Win a FREE Ride in a Police Car just by shoplifting from this store.**

   Lucky Winners will also get their name in the newspaper for their friends and family to see!

   Won't Mom & Dad be proud?

   You could see this sign
   A ☐ in a supermarket.
   B ☐ at a police station.
   C ☐ at a taxi stand.
   D ☐ in a lift.

3.

CENTRAL CRIMINAL COURT

SECURITY NOTICE

IN THE INTERESTS OF SAFETY & SECURITY

ALL PERSONS ENTERING THE COURT WILL BE SEARCHED

PLEASE BE READY TO CO-OPERATE WITH THE SECURITY TEAM. *Thank you!*

A ☐ You should apply here if you want to work on the security team.

B ☐ For safety reasons the courtroom will be searched before session.

C ☐ You are not allowed to enter the building during court hours.

D ☐ When entering this building be ready for a security check.

4. **MTV Open Casting Call in Chicago for Teens**

MTV is having an **open casting call** for high school dropouts for a new reality show. MTV is casting for 20 high school dropouts who will be given another chance to take classes again. The teachers will be people who are the top of their fields. The teens will also be able to speak with people from several organizations about returning to school and entering the job force.
With this show MTV hopes to get the 20 students excited about school again.

For a new reality TV show MTV is looking for

A ☐ students who have always loved going to school.

B ☐ young people who have left school without any qualifications.

C ☐ teachers who are good at motivating young people.

D ☐ organizations that offer jobs to high school students.

5.

LOYALTY CARD

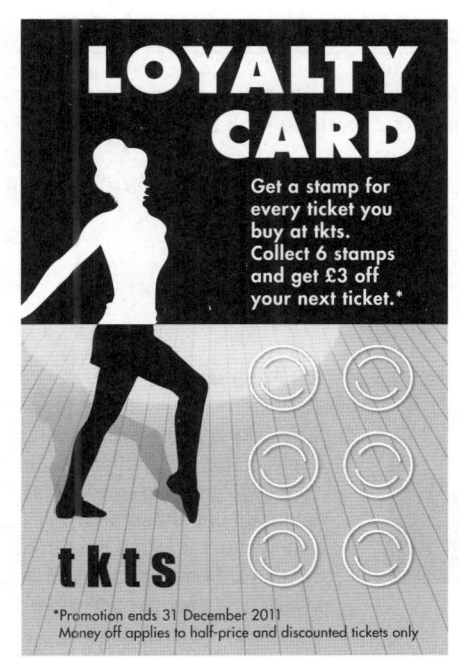

Get a stamp for every ticket you buy at tkts. Collect 6 stamps and get £3 off your next ticket.*

tkts

*Promotion ends 31 December 2011
Money off applies to half-price and discounted tickets only

A ☐ Buy six tickets and get one free.

B ☐ When you have six stamps, you will get a reduction.

C ☐ Your loyalty card costs £3.

D ☐ This card is a group ticket for six people.

Reading Part 2: Activities in Edinburgh

- These tourists (a–e) are looking for two activities to do in Edinburgh.
- First read the information about the tourists, then look at the activities (A–G) on the next page.
- In each case (a–e) find the **two** activities the tourists can do. Write the letters of the activities in the boxes next to the tourists' names.
- Some of the activities can be chosen more than once.

No.	Activity 1	Activity 2		The tourists
6/7				a) **Eiji Fujimura** Eiji is from Tokyo, Japan, and he is very fond of the arts from his home country. So wherever he is, he enjoys going to events that celebrate Japanese arts. Mr Fujimura is also a big fan of the Royal Family and would like to see how they used to travel when they were at sea.
8/9				b) **Deirdre and Brenda** These two elderly ladies are still young at heart and they like events for and/or about children and young people. They hope to find a museum that does not cost anything. In the evening they're planning to spend some time in a trendy area of the city and go for a drink.
10/11				c) **Heidi K. Lumm** Heidi usually travels alone but she does not like exploring sights on her own. She prefers a guide to tell her interesting things. She is also very interested in fashion. That is why she would like to find the part of the city where she can check out the latest trends.

2013-10

12/13				d)	**Russel Perry** Russel lives in a very busy area of his hometown with lots of shops and bars so he would like to have some peace and quiet and enjoy nature when he is away. He is also very interested in the arts, especially in classical music.
14/15				e)	**McBergers** Clive and Helen McBerger are spending the weekend in Edinburgh with their children. On Saturday they would like to learn something about the history of Edinburgh. Since they are all interested in astronomy and science, they would like to go to an exhibittion or a museum on Sunday before they leave the city around 1 pm.

A) **Edinburgh Castle**

No visit to Edinburgh is complete without a visit to Edinburgh Castle, and once you have ventured up to the highest parts of Edinburgh Castle's structure, you will be overwhelmed by the spectacular views of Edinburgh afforded from this Scottish "Castle of Castles".

A complimentary guided tour of the castle is offered by experienced and well-informed stewards. Experienced guides with a great knowledge of Edinburgh's past look forward to sharing their stories with you.

Opening times: Daily 9.30 am – 6.00 pm

Admission: Adult: £15.00; Child: £8.50; Child under 5: FREE

B) Our Dynamic Earth

Our Dynamic Earth takes you on a journey through our planet's past, present and future, with interactive exhibits and impressive technology, including a 4D and 3D experience. Beginning with the Big Bang, children and adults alike can witness the creation of the Earth, follow the planet through its evolution and even catch glimpses of its future. Dynamic Earth presents all aspects of the planet we live in.

Opening times: 10.00 to 17.30 daily (last entry 1 hour 30 mins before closing)

Admission: Adults: £10.80; Children (3–15): £7.80; Students: £9.50

C) The Museum of Childhood

The Museum of Childhood is a fun day out for the whole family. Young people can learn about the children of the past and see a fantastic range of toys and games, while adults enjoy a trip down memory lane.

Young people and adults will enjoy finding out about growing up through the ages, from toys and games to health and school days. Hands-on activities, together with our fantastic museum shop, help to make your visit a memorable one.

Opening times: Monday – Saturday 10 am – 5 pm; Sunday 12 pm – 5 pm.

Admission: Admission is free, but donations are welcome.

D) George Street

From fashionista's favourite Harvey Nichols and designer shops to star studded jewellers, George Street has it all going on. And when day turns to night, the street comes alive with partygoers who flock to the area's many stylish bars. This district's vision is to ensure that Edinburgh city centre excels as a place to work, a place to do business, a place to shop and a place to visit. Welcome to Edinburgh's most celebrated shopping area.

E) Edinburgh Music Festival

Experience the unique atmosphere of Edinburgh in August during an unforgettable three weeks of the very best in international opera, music, theatre, dance and visual arts.

This year's festival celebrates the vibrant and diverse cultures of Asia with the finest artists from countries and regions including China, India, Japan, Korea, Taiwan and Vietnam joining others from around the world to explore our shared passions, all against the backdrop of Scotland's stunning capital city.

F) The Royal Botanic Garden

The Royal Botanic Garden Edinburgh was established in 1670 and during the twentieth century acquired three Regional Gardens – the mountainous Benmore in Argyll; Dawyck in the wooded hills of the Scottish Borders and Logan on the Gulf Stream-warmed southern peninsula of Dumfries & Galloway. Refresh your senses and explore the riches of the green kingdom at one of the world's finest botanic gardens.

Opening times: 10 am to 6 pm

G) Royal Yacht Britannia

This magnificent ship has played host to some of the most famous people in the world. But, above all, she was home to Her Majesty The Queen and the Royal Family. Now in Edinburgh you are welcome on board to discover the heart and soul of this most special of royal residences. A must-see tourist attraction in Edinburgh's historic port of Leith.

Opening times in the summer: 9.30 am – 4.30 pm

Admission: Adults £ 11; Children (5–17) £ 7; Families (2 adults and up to 3 children) £ 32.50

Quellennachweis: A) Adapted from: Edinburgh Media, URL: http://www.edinburghcastle.biz/; B) Adapted from: Our Dynamic Earth, URL: http://www.dynamicearth.co.uk/visitors/whatisode;C) Adapted from: City of Edinburgh Council, URL: http://www.edinburgh museums.org.uk/Venues/ Museum-of-Childhood; D) Adapted from: George Street Association, URL: http://www.edinburghgeorge street.co.uk/; E) Adapted from: Edinburgh International Festival Society, URL: http://www.eif.co.uk/; F) Adapted from: Royal Botanic Garden Edinburgh, URL:; http://www.rbge.org.uk/the-gardens/home; G) Adapted from: The Royal Yacht Britannia, URL: http://www. royalyachtbritannia.co.uk/plan-your-visit/the-britannia-experience

Reading Part 3: Learning from a Scary Guy

- Read the text and the statements on the opposite page.
- Put a tick (✓) in the box next to the correct answer.
- Only one answer is correct in each case.

1　He wears sunglasses and a leather jacket. Piercings cover his face, tattoos cover his body and his facial hair is died a bright yellow. His name is The Scary Guy. When he walks into the gym of Jaffrey-Rindge Middle School on Thursday morning, all the students fall silent and stare at him. Scary Guy knows exactly how people are judging
5　him, thinking he is a biker or a wrestler and a potentially dangerous person. All of this is based on the way he looks. But by the end of his presentation, they are lining up to give him hugs.

　　In fact, Scary Guy was a tattoo artist, and before that he was a computer salesman. Before that, he shot baby portraits for a living. He got his first tattoo at the age of 30
10　and now has tattoos that cover an estimated 85 % of his body. He has added them over the years as a reflection of his life. They are what he calls modern tribalism and reflect events he has experienced from humorous to stressful. There is a tattoo of a guy who represents his former life in the computer business called "Yuppiecide". Other tattoos represent his own art or designs he thinks look cool. The change came for him
15　in 1998, when he legally changed his name in an Arizona court from Earl Kenneth Kaufmann to The Scary Guy. He hit the road, sold his tattoo shops and decided it was his mission to teach people how to create love and peace. Now Scary Guy gives 700 live performances per year. "This is a mission," Scary Guy says. "I only have so much time. I want to reach as many people as I can before I die."

20　In residence at Jaffrey-Rindge Middle School for Thursday and Friday, Scary Guy speaks before the entire school, individual classes, a group of teachers and a group of community members. Throughout his time at the school, Scary Guy teaches that people need to understand that hateful speech says more about the speaker than about the person it is directed at. "You have to imagine in New York City someone looking like
25　this walking down the street," Scary Guy says. "They look at me like, 'There's another lunatic. What an idiot. Who would want to do that to themselves?' That's them, not me."

　　Scary Guy's physical appearance is an important aspect of his presentation. In a world full of violent images on television, on the Internet and in other media, he is
30　able to get people's attention. The middle school students were not attracted by his presentation because he is a nice guy with a good message, but they were blown away by his image and his message combined. Once he has their attention, however, and he is able to get his message across, the tattoos and the rest of his image melt away.

　　Ryan Earley, principal of Jaffrey-Rindge Middle School, says he heard about
35　Scary Guy from health teacher Michelle Durand, who had been trying to bring him to

the school for seven years. "His message is equivalent with what we're trying to coach in our school with that low level bullying," Earley says. He continues to say that they deal with – rather than ignore – the beginning stages of bullying before it escalates. According to Earley, Scary Guy's program was a success. "I was astounded at the interest by our entire student body," Earley says. "Scary stated this was the first time after a performance that audience members made a line to give him a hug goodbye or a kind word." That happened with Scary Guy's presentation to the eighth grade class, which went 45 minutes longer than planned.

In addition to the formal sessions, Scary Guy sat down together with Earley, assistant principal Robert Clark and school behavior specialist Taylor Ratcliffe to talk to a student identified as an at-risk student. "I think it was very meaningful to show the individual there were three people in the school who cared," Earley says.

In the coming weeks, the middle school will make Scary Guy's message part of their teaching program. This includes not using any hateful speech for seven days. Earley says the school will also look to bring Scary Guy back regularly every few years. "His message is so prepared and so meaningful that after the first couple of minutes, I didn't see the tattoos or the piercings," Earley says. "I just heard meaning coming from him. He connects with every individual because everyone can relate to areas of love and pain and, at the same time, the desire to change the world and empower each other to move past hate."

based on: Monadnock Ledger-Transcript, URL: http://www.ledgertranscript.com/article/learning-from-scary-guy (24. 6. 2011) and the article "The Scary Guy" from Wikipedia, the Free Encyclopedia, licensed under CC-BY-SA 3.0 Unported, URL: http://en.wikipedia.org/wiki/The_Scary_Guy (07.09.2011)

16. Scary Guy's outward appearance makes
    - A ☐ him look like a celebrity.
    - B ☐ him look dangerous.
    - C ☐ the students at the school cheer loudly.
    - D ☐ all of them (A + B + C)

17. In the past Scary Guy
    - A ☐ sold computers.
    - B ☐ wrote a book on modern tribalism.
    - C ☐ killed somebody.
    - D ☐ both B + C

18. The tattoos on Scary Guy's body
    - A ☐ now add up to 30.
    - B ☐ show phases and events in his life.
    - C ☐ started off as a joke.
    - D ☐ were designed by "Yuppiecide".

19. In 1998 Scary Guy
    A ☐ changed his life.
    B ☐ had to go to prison.
    C ☐ joined the peace movement.
    D ☐ nearly died.

20. At JR Middle School[1] Scary Guy
    A ☐ talks to each student individually.
    B ☐ explains that hateful speech shows the speaker's character.
    C ☐ talks about his future life in New York City.
    D ☐ tells his listeners that he sees himself as a lunatic.

    1 JR Middle School = Jaffrey-Rindge Middle School

21. Scary Guy first attracts the students' attention because
    A ☐ of the way he looks.
    B ☐ they know him from television.
    C ☐ of the violent pictures he shows.
    D ☐ he is a nice person.

22. The principal of JR Middle School, Ryan Earley,
    A ☐ told a health teacher to interview Scary Guy.
    B ☐ is worried about the bullying among his colleagues.
    C ☐ believes in Scary Guy's message.
    D ☐ met Scary Guy 7 years ago.

23. Scary Guy's program at JR Middle School
    A ☐ lasted 45 minutes.
    B ☐ was designed for at-risk students.
    C ☐ was successful with the students.
    D ☐ both A + B

24. JR Middle School is planning to
    A ☐ integrate Scary Guy's ideas into the lessons.
    B ☐ punish students for using hateful speech.
    C ☐ invite Scary Guy every year.
    D ☐ all of them (A + B + C)

25. Which saying sums up the message of the text best?
    A ☐ Don't throw the baby out with the bath water
    B ☐ Attack is the best form of defence.
    C ☐ Don't judge a book by its cover.
    D ☐ Better late than never.

Reading: Candidate Answer Sheet   Name: _____

For students: Put a tick (✓) in the correct box.

Part 1

Number	A	B	C	D
1				
2				
3				
4				
5				

/ 5 P

Part 2 (Edinburgh)

Number	Name	A	B	C	D	E	F	G
6/7	a) Eiji Fujimura							
8/9	b) Deidre and Brenda							
10/11	c) Heidi K. Lumm							
12/13	d) Russel Perry							
14/15	e) McBergers							

/ 10 P

Part 3

Number	A	B	C	D
16				
17				
18				
19				
20				
21				
22				
23				
24				
25				

/ 10 P

/ 25 P

2013-17

Writing Part 1: International Work Camp

You want to help in a social project and work together with young people from all over the world.

- Complete the application form below.
- You must fill in each item. You may use your imagination.
- Just use **keywords** *(Stichwörter)*, do not write complete sentences.
- Remember: Correct spelling is important!

Work Camp Application

You are interested in working for an international project? Then we need to know more about you. Please fill in this questionnaire to help us find the right project for you.

(1) Name: _____
    Age: _____
    Sex: _____

    1 P

(2) What kind of work are you interested in?
    _____

    1 P

(3) What languages do you speak? (Name two)
    - _____
    - _____

    1 P

(4) What do you like doing in your free time?
    _____

    1 P

(5) Which country would you like to go to?
    _____

    1 P

/5 P

Writing Part 2: Social Networks

- Read what Gloria has written.
- Then write back, answering all of her questions.
- You must write a minimum of 100 words. Do not use Internet slang.

E-pinion

Search the Web   ◯ go

E-pinion ▶ Community ▶ Public	User Name _____	☐ Remember Me?
.... 🗁 **social networking sites**	Password _____	◯ Log in.

| Register | Help | Members List | Calendar | Arcade | Articles | Today's Post | Journal ▽ | Search ▽ |

Name: Gloria (15)
Joined E-pinion: February 2013
Location: Swansea, Wales

Hey guys,

I've got a real problem with my boyfriend. He spends so much time on social networking sites that he doesn't have any time left for me. Maybe you've got some good advice. How long do you spend chatting online with your friends and when do you do it? What do you think of social networks? I know they have lots of good sides, but they can cause some real problems, too.
What can I do to get my boyfriend away from his computer? Please give me some ideas.

Gloria

Hi Gloria,

_____
_____
_____
_____
_____
_____
_____

Inhalt: [/5 P] Sprache: [/5 P] Gesamt: [/10 P]

2013-19

Writing Part 3: Two Tickets

T-Hall

Klettern ist mehr als nur ein Sport – die T-Hall ist mehr als nur ein Ort, um ihn auszuüben. Hier können Sie unter Anleitung und in freundlicher Atmosphäre das Klettern erlernen und erleben.

Wir bieten eine Vielzahl an Kursen, die von professionellen Trainerinnen und Trainern betreut werden und an denen Sie ohne Vorkenntnisse teilnehmen können.

Unsere 7 m bis 12 m hohen Kletterwände laden auf über 1 800 m² mit mehr als 200 Routen zu den ersten Schritten ein und bieten gleichermaßen herausfordernde Schwierigkeiten für fortgeschrittene Kletterer. Kraftraum, Sauna und Bistro runden das Erlebnis in der T-Hall ab.

Thiemannstr. 1
12059 Berlin
Mo – Fr 10.00 – 24.00 Uhr
Sa, So, Feiertage 10.00 – 22.00 Uhr

Berliner Unterwelten

Erleben Sie Berliner Stadtgeschichte aus einer ungewöhnlichen Perspektive!

Wir bieten seit 1999 regelmäßige Führungen durch unterirdische Bauwerke an. Verkehrsgünstig gelegen, haben wir an verschiedenen Orten in der Stadt mehrere Touren für Sie zusammengestellt, die durch geheimnisumwitterte und lange Zeit in Vergessenheit geratene Bunker- und Verkehrsanlagen des Berliner Untergrunds führen. Herzlich willkommen in der Berliner Unterwelt!

Generell wird bei allen Touren die Mitnahme wärmender Kleidung (z. B. Pullover) empfohlen, da es in den unterirdischen Anlagen auch in den heißen Sommermonaten recht kühl bleibt. Die Führungen sind in verschiedenen Sprachen verfügbar.

Startort abhängig von der gewählten Tour

Info-Telefon: (030) 499 105-18

Batman Live

Der erfolgreichste Comic-Held aller Zeiten, Batman, steht im Mittelpunkt einer gigantischen Arena-Produktion, die den Zuschauer ganz in den Bann eines aktions- und spannungsgeladenen Geschehens zieht.

Batman Live ist furioses, magisches und vollkommen neues Entertainment, das Bühnenillusionen, Spezialeffekte, tollkühne Akrobatik und atemberaubende Stunts zu einem dreidimensionalen Live-Erlebnis verbindet.

Batman Live, in Szene gesetzt nach Hauptmotiven der Originalvorlagen, präsentiert den Superhelden und seinen wichtigsten Gefährten sowie erbitterte Gegenspieler in ihrer ganz eigenen Welt. Noch niemals zuvor wurden Gotham City, die Bathöhle und das Arkham Asylum in einer visuell so atemberaubenden Weise zum Leben erweckt.

---

1. Adapted from: T-Hall Kletteranlagen GmbH Berlin, URL: http://www.diekletterhalle.de/
2. Adapted from: Berliner Unterwelten e.V. URL: http://berliner-unterwelten.de/fuehrungen.3.0.html
3. Adapted from: CTS EVENTIM AG, URL: http://www.eventim.de/batman-live.html?affiliate=TUG&doc=artistPages/overview&fun=artist&action=overview&kuid=455696

Writing Part 3: Two Tickets

As a present for your birthday your parents want to give you two tickets for an event. You would like to go there with your Irish friend who is coming to visit you for a week.
- Read the three texts.
- Choose **two** events/activities.
- Write an e-mail to your friend telling him/her about the two events/activities you have chosen.
- For each one of them say what kind of event/activity it is and mention at least two more aspects that are important.
- **Do not translate word for word**, just give the main information used in these texts.
- Write complete sentences and use correct English.

To: _____@hotmail.com

Ref: Let's go out

Hey _____,

I've just got a super birthday present – two tickets for an event of my choice. And that's something that we could do together when you are here. Here are the two events I find most interesting.

_____
_____
_____
_____
_____

Which of the two would you like to go to? Tell me what you think.
☺ _____

Inhalt: / 6 P   Sprache: / 4 P   Gesamt: / 10 P

Lösungsvorschläge

Listening Part 1: Voicemail Messages

Message One

Hey Emily, it's me – Nora. Looks like it's not going to rain tomorrow after all, so our class barbecue can go ahead as planned. And thank heavens for that. Grilled meat is so much better than cold sandwiches! We've got to set up that big grill, so let's meet Larry and Joe in front of the cafeteria at 5 o'clock instead of 6, OK? I've already got 3 bags of coal and the boys are bringing steaks for the 4 of us. So why don't you bring some sausages? Call back if you want. Bye!

1. C
   Hinweis: "... let's meet ... at 5 o'clock ..." (Z. 4)

2. C
   Hinweis: "So why don't you bring some sausages?" (Z. 5/6)

Message Two

Hey Mark, Sam here. Hope you're feeling better and haven't spent the whole afternoon learning for that Math test tomorrow. I just wanted to let you know that Ms Stewart is ill and won't be in tomorrow. So instead of a double period of Math, we'll have Geography with Ms Lambert for the first period, then Chemistry with grumpy old Dr Chisolm. But, thank God, after that we'll have a double period of Art with that cute new teacher Mr Richy, which will save my day! See ya!

3. B
   Hinweis: "... Geography ... for the first period, then Chemistry ... after that we'll have a double period of Art ..." (Z. 4–6)

4. B
   Hinweis: "... a double period of Art with that cute new teacher Mr Richy, which will save my day!" (Z. 5/6)

Listening Part 2: Radio Ads

Ad 1: Diving Buddy School

1 *(heavy breathing)* Buddy Dive Course is the beginning of your way in scuba diving education. During the training you'll get a basic knowledge in scuba diving skills, which after receiving a certificate allow you to independently plan and perform dives with a partner. Almost immediately after signing up for the course,
5 you'll be able to perform your first scuba dive. The PADI Dive Education System will ensure you'll get a full-founded knowledge and skills before receiving a certificate. Five lectures, five confined water classes and four open-water dives. To enroll you must be over 15 years old and able to swim 200 meters without fence or 300 meters in the fence. After obtaining the certificate of open-water diver,
10 you'll be able to use various diving centers. Sign up today and join us at the party ... *(completely out of breath, breathing in heavily, then breathing very quickly)*

http://adsoftheworld.com/media/radio/buddy_diving_school_breath [17. 08. 2011]

5. B
Hinweis: "Buddy Dive Course is the beginning of your way in scuba diving education. During the training you'll get a basic knowledge in scuba diving skills ..." (Z. 1–3); "Sign up today and join us at the party ..." (Z. 10/11)

Ad 2: Nebraska Cat

1 You may have heard about our recent promotion where every student who sold back text books received a ... cat. We apologize! In particular to Sean Nelson, whose face may never look the same. And to all those who witnessed the litter incident, well, nobody should have to smell that. Instead: Thanks to our nation-
5 wide buy-back program, we'll go back to offering the most cash for your used books, guaranteed ... as soon as we replace the carpet. *(meow)*
Only Nebraska Book Store, 1300 Q Street. For students who like money.

Archrival USA

6. C
Hinweis: "Thanks to our nation-wide buy-back program, we'll go back to offering the most cash for your used books ..." (Z. 4–6)

Ad 3: Time Machine

1 SPEAKER 1: Joe, it's a time machine, just press a button and you'll go back in time.
SPEAKER 2: No way!
SPEAKER 1: Joe, it's a time machine, just press a button and you'll go back in time.
SPEAKER 2: No way!

SPEAKER 1: Joe, it's a time machine, just press a button and you'll go back in time.
SPEAKER 2: No way!
SPEAKER 1: Joe, it's a time machine, just press a button and you'll go back in time.
SPEAKER 2: No way!
SPEAKER 1: Joe, it's a time machine, just press a button and you'll go back in time.
SPEAKER 2: No way!
SPEAKER 3: Is it science or science fiction? Come find out at the expo for young scientist national files. University of Pretoria Sports Centre. Friday 3 October, 3–5 pm and Saturday 4 October, 8–12 am. Visit exposcience.co.za for more information.

http://adsoftheworld.com/media/radio/eskom_young_scientists_expo_time_machine [17. 08. 2011]

7. A

Hinweis: "Come find out at the expo for young scientist national files. University of Pretoria ..." (Z. 11/12)

Ad 4: Flu Bug

ANNOUNCER: Welcome to Flu Bug University. We now join Professor Green's Influenza Germ 101 class.
PROFESSOR: Attention! What are the best ways to spread the flu?
FLU BUG: Make sure people sneeze in their hands and forget to wash them!
PROFESSOR: Excellent!
FLU BUG: Get people to go to work and to school when they're SICK!
PROFESSOR: Perfect!
FLU BUG: Keep people from getting flu shots!
PROFESSOR: RIGHT! If people do that, those things will kill us flu bugs for sure!
ANNOUNCER: This flu season, don't let the flu bug you.
Brought to you by the Kansas Department of Health and Environment.

Kansas Department of Health and Environment, URL: http://www.kdheks.gov/flu/FluBugU.htm

8. C

Hinweis: "This flu season, don't let the flu bug you." (Z. 10)
Everything the Flu Bug says is ironic, which means it is just the opposite of what you should do to protect yourself.

Listening Part 3: The Globe Theatre

*"For never was a story of more woe
Than this of Juliet and her Romeo."
(Thunderous applause ...)*

GUIDE: With these final words from William Shakespeare's tragic love story "Romeo and Juliet" I would like to welcome you to London's new Globe Theatre. The plays of Britain's most famous author William Shakespeare are known and performed all over the world, from Munich to Mumbai, from Tokyo to Toronto.

The building you are in now is not Shakespeare's original Globe Theatre, which was torn down more than 350 years ago. How terrible that must have been for people at a time when going to the theatre was as popular as going to the cinema today. In those days everybody – rich and poor, young and old – went to the theatre to enjoy themselves. When in 1989 the decision was made to rebuild the old Globe Theatre, the builders wanted it to look exactly like Shakespeare's original. It took eight years before the new Globe could be officially opened by Queen Elizabeth II in 1997.

The area directly in front of the stage where you are standing was the cheapest part of the theatre where people only had to pay one penny. But as you can see there are no seats here, so to watch a play these so-called groundlings had to stand on the ground for more than three hours. Sometimes there were up to 500 people crowded into this central area and on hot summer days these "groundlings" were also called "stinkards", for obvious reasons.

But if you wanted to get away from the smell and be a bit more comfortable, you paid two pennies to sit in the covered galleries all along the back of the theatre. Rich aristocrats would often pay a lot more to have a chair on the side of the Globe stage itself.

In Shakespeare's day the audiences did not behave in the same way as an audience would in a theatre today. During the performance they would eat, drink, talk and laugh. Aristocrats who sat at the side of the stage were often heard discussing the play or making comments about other people in the theatre. Although the audience would often clap and cheer, the groundlings would also boo, hiss and throw things at the actors if they did not like what they were watching. But sometimes members of the audience would forget that what they saw on stage was not real like young Molly Putnam when she was watching a new play called "Romeo and Juliet":

MOLLY: It's the most romantic play I've ever seen *(she sighs)* – handsome Romeo – now secretly married to his beautiful Juliet ...

(excited) But wait, wait a minute. Romeo, what are you doing with that bottle? Put it down! Don't drink that poison! Juliet's not dead, she's only sleeping! *(Molly starts sobbing, then sounds of sobbing of other people fade in).*
OTHER VOICES: He's dying! / Oh, why didn't you listen? …
GUIDE: Young Molly was so excited that she even forgot that the role of Juliet was being played by a man. In those days women were not allowed to act on stage, so all female roles were performed by young men in women's clothes.
If we walk up the side stairs onto the Globe stage itself, you will get an idea of what it must have felt like for an actor looking down on all those faces … Let's listen to what Henry Condell, one of Shakespeare's main actors, has to say about the groundlings:
HENRY: The groundlings? Ha! They can really get out of control sometimes. Once when I was playing evil King Richard III, someone shouted, 'Down with the king! Off with his head!' Others joined in by throwing rotten tomatoes and cabbages at me. Some of them even started climbing up onto the stage, but when my "soldiers" pointed their swords at them, they backed down. Having to act in front of groundlings is not easy. But still, they bring in money and we need all we can get. We have to perform a play at least three times to pay for everything. The first day pays for theatre expenses, especially costumes. With the money from the second day, we actors get paid and only on the third day does Shakespeare finally earn something for the play he has written.
GUIDE: Yes, life was not easy for actors in those days. But Londoners loved their theatre and with all the beautiful costumes and wonderful special effects it was never boring. Special effects? Sure! They fired a real cannon, used real (sheep's) blood and had real corpses *(fading out)* hanging from the rafters …

Based on:
1. Shakespeare Resource Center at www.bardweb.net/globe.html.
2. Mabillard, Amanda: The Globe. Shakespeare Online. 20. 08. 2000. www.shakespeare-online.com/theatre/globe.html
3. www.globe-theatre.org.uk
4. www.elizabethan-era.org.uk/elizabethan-theatre-audiences.htm [August 17, 2011]

9. Yes
   Hinweis: "… at a time when going to the theatre was as popular as going to the cinema today." (Z. 11/12)

10. No
    Hinweis: "When in 1989 the decision was made to rebuild the old Globe Theatre …" (Z. 13/14)

11. Yes
    Hinweis: "… to watch a play these so-called groundlings had to stand on the ground for more than three hours." (Z. 19/20)

12. Yes
   Hinweis: "... on hot summer days these 'groundlings' were also called 'stinkards', for obvious reasons." (Z. 21/22)
13. No
   Hinweis: "During the performance they would eat, drink ..." (Z. 28)
14. Yes
   Hinweis: "Although the audience would often clap and cheer, the groundlings would also boo, hiss and throw things at the actors ..." (Z. 30–32)
15. Yes
   Hinweis: "But sometimes members of the audience would forget that what they saw on stage was not real like young Molly Putnam ..." (Z. 33/34)
   "Put it down! Don't drink that poison! Juliet's not dead, she's only sleeping!" (Z. 39)
16. Yes
   Hinweis: "... Juliet was being played by a man. In those days women were not allowed to act on stage, so all female roles were performed by young men in women's clothes." (Z. 42–44)
17. Yes
   Hinweis: "Having to act in front of groundlings is not easy." (Z. 53/54)
18. No
   Hinweis: "... on the third day does Shakespeare finally earn something for the play he has written." (Z. 57–59)

Listening Part 4: Extreme Sports

PRESENTER: Welcome to *Talk of the Time* with your host Alison Freeman. Today our topic is extreme sports. Though traditional sports like football and hockey aren't going out of style, the world of extreme sports is growing fast. Years ago everyone was talking about bungee jumping. These days an extreme sport called BASE jumping is in the headlines. To tell us more about this extreme sport we have invited Greg Moore, a BASE jumper from Chicago. Welcome Greg.
GREG: Great to be here, Alison.
PRESENTER: And we have Adam Sweeney, a rescuer, who has risked his own life on many occasions to save the lives of other people.
ADAM: Hello, good afternoon.
PRESENTER: Then we also have Marietta Collins, a sports psychologist, who will give us some insight into one of the world's most dangerous sports.
MARIETTA: Pleased to be here.

PRESENTER: Greg, would you tell our listeners what BASE jumping is?

GREG: Well, the word BASE – B-A-S-E – stands for Building, Antennae, Span, Earth. These are the objects that people jump from. BASE jumpers will jump with a parachute off any tall building, bridge or cliff and they've even jumped from the Eiffel Tower and the Empire State Building.

PRESENTER: Unbelievable! Obviously for BASE jumpers jumping out of a plane and falling at a speed of over 100 mph is not exciting enough. I guess you have to make freefalling more interesting by jumping from a very low height, which gives you only a few seconds to open the parachute, and hardly any time at all to deal with any problems. But the numbers speak for themselves: There is one death for every sixty jumps. Don't you consider that extremely dangerous?

GREG: Yes, it is really dangerous if you're not extremely fit and well-trained in skydiving.

PRESENTER: But if it's so dangerous, why do you do it?

GREG: It's fun! ... And the high element of risk makes me feel really great, makes me feel alive! I'm also in it for challenge; I want to test how far I can go. Sometimes I get scared, but that just makes me fight more to overcome my fears.

PRESENTER: Marietta, as a sports psychologist, can you tell us why extreme sportsmen and -women enjoy putting themselves in such danger?

MARIETTA: Well, as Greg says, they do it to get a thrill, to feel alive. It's all about adrenaline. You see, in a dangerous situation, adrenaline gets into the blood system, the heart starts to pump harder, the blood pressure rises. The body is preparing the muscles to fight or to run away, a response known as fight-or-flight. But when a person knows he's not in danger – is NOT being chased by a Rottweiler or a hungry lion – this fluttery feeling can be fun and exciting. That's why this adrenaline rush is seen as a very positive part of the extreme sport experience.

PRESENTER: But things can also go very wrong for the BASE jumper ... a change in the weather, the parachute doesn't open ... That's when other people – rescuers, like Adam – have to be called in. Adam, what in the world attracted you to the job of being a rescuer in the first place?

ADAM: Well, I'm an outdoor person and I like the challenge of being able to save people's lives. That's why I became a member of SR – the Search and Rescue team. I love the constant training we do; it keeps me fit. And in times of stress I can keep a clear head, which is of absolute importance in extreme situations. Sure, the job is risky, but a monotonous 9-to-5 office job would kill me.

PRESENTER: And how far are you willing to go to risk your own life for others?

ADAM: There is always a certain amount of pressure on us to do everything possible to rescue someone in trouble. I'd help rescue anyone anywhere, but I must say I have absolutely no sympathy for extreme sportsmen who not only endanger their own lives, but also ours and the lives of other innocent people. I don't think BASE jumping is a sport at all. It's a high risk activity, and can cause DEATH.

GREG: Hmpf ... maybe we should just wrap ourselves up in plastic bubble packaging for the rest of our lives. Then we'd all be safe from falling and injuring ourselves.

MARIETTA: Well, in a way Greg, you and Adam are quite similar!

ADAM / GREG: No way!

MARIETTA: Both of you are risk takers. You, Adam, are what we call a pro-social risk taker, someone who helps other people in dangerous situations, like a fireman or a policeman. And you, Greg, belong to the group we call ludic risk takers, people who take risks just for fun.

ADAM: Okay, but the question is: Where does the fun end? What really makes me angry is how some people in the BASE jumping subculture can be so cold and cynical. They've got no respect for other jumpers and they don't respect the rescue team either. I've seen some of them continue their jump while injured jumpers are being carried away!

GREG: It's guys like that who have given us a bad name and fill the papers with these horror stories ...

PRESENTER: And that will be our topic after a short break "How BASE jumping is presented in the media" ...

Based on: One giant leap as a base jumper hurtles himself off the world's tallest building. In: Daily Mail, 13 Dec 2007; Kyanna Sutton: Kids and Extreme Sports. In: familyeducation [15.09.2011].

19. B

Hinweis: ... *the word BASE – B-A-S-E – stands for Building, Antennae, Span, Earth. These are the objects that people jump from." (Z. 16/17)*

20. B

Hinweis: "... more interesting by jumping from a very low height, which gives you only a few seconds to open the parachute, and hardly any time at all to deal with any problems." (Z. 22–24)

21. C

Hinweis: "I want to test how far I can go." (Z. 31)

22. A

Hinweis: "It's all about adrenaline ... The body is preparing the muscles to fight or to run away, a response known as fight-or-flight." (Z. 35–39)

23. C

Hinweis: "... I like the challenge of being able to save people's lives." (Z. 47/48) "I love the constant training we do; it keeps me fit. And in times of stress I can keep a clear head ..." (Z. 49/50)

24. A
   Hinweis: "... who not only endanger their own lives, but also ours and the lives of other innocent people." (Z. 55–57)

25. A
   Hinweis: "Both of you are risk takers. You, Adam, are what we call a prosocial risk taker, someone who helps other people in dangerous situations ... And you, Greg, belong to the group we call ludic risk takers, people who take risks just for fun." (Z. 64–67)

Reading Part 1: Short Texts

1. B
   Hinweis: "I need three models ..."

2. A
   Hinweis: "... just by shoplifting from this store."
   Hier musst du den Text besonders genau lesen und darfst dich nicht von dem Polizeiauto in die Irre führen lassen. Der Text ist ironisch gemeint: Natürlich kann man die Fahrt im Polizeiauto nicht wirklich gewinnen, sondern man wird von der Polizei mitgenommen, wenn man einen Ladendiebstahl begeht.

3. D
   Hinweis: "All persons entering the court will be searched."

4. B
   Hinweis: "... open casting call for high school dropouts for a new reality show."

5. B
   Hinweis: "Collect 6 stamps and get £3 off your next ticket."

Reading Part 2: Activities in Edinburgh

6./7. E, G
   Hinweis: Eiji Fujimura: "... enjoys going to events that celebrate Japanese arts."
   → Activity E: "... celebrates the vibrant and diverse cultures of Asia with the finest artists ..."
   Eiji Fujimura: "... a big fan of the Royal Family and would like to see how they used to travel when they were at sea."
   → Activity G: "Royal Yacht Britannia ... was home to Her Majesty The Queen and the Royal Family."

8./9. C, D

Hinweis: Deirdre and Brenda: "... still young at heart and they like events for and/or about children and young people. They hope to find a museum that does not cost anything."
→ Activity C: "The Museum of Childhood"; "Admission is free ..."
Deirdre and Brenda: "... to spend some time in a trendy area of the city and go for a drink."
→ Activity D: "... partygoers who flock to the area's many stylish bars."

10./11. A, D

Hinweis: Heidi K. Lumm: "She prefers a guide to tell her interesting things."
→ Activity A: "A complimentary guided tour of the castle ..."
Heidi K. Lumm: "... interested in fashion ... would like to find the part of the city where she can check out the latest trends."
→ Activity D: "From fashionista's favourite Harvey Nichols and designer shops ..."

12./13. E, F

Hinweis: Russel Perry: "... very interested in the arts, especially in classical music."
→ Activity E: "... the very best in international opera, music ..."
Russel Perry: "... would like to have some peace and quiet and enjoy nature when he is away."
→ Activity F: "Refresh your senses and explore the riches of the green kingdom ..."

14./15. A, B

Hinweis: McBergers: "... would like to learn something about the history of Edinburgh."
→ Activity A: "Experienced guides with a great knowledge of Edinburgh's past look forward to sharing their stories with you."
McBergers: "... interested in astronomy and science, they would like to go to an exhibition or a museum ..."
→ Activity B: "Our Dynamic Earth takes you on a journey through our planet's past, present and future, with interactive exhibits and impressive technology ..."

Reading Part 3: Learning from a Scary Guy

16. B
    Hinweis: "... thinking he is ... a potentially dangerous person. All of this is based on the way he looks." (Z. 5/6)

17. A
    Hinweis: "... before that he was a computer salesman." (Z. 8)

18. B
    Hinweis: "... as a reflection of his life ... reflect events he has experienced ..." (Z. 11/12)

19. A
    Hinweis: "The change came for him in 1998 ..." (Z. 14/15)

20. B
    Hinweis: "... teaches that people need to understand that hateful speech says more about the speaker than about the person it is directed at." (Z. 22–24)

21. A
    Hinweis: "The middle school students were not attracted by his presentation because he is a nice guy with a good message, but they were blown away by his image and his message combined." (Z. 30–32)

22. C
    Hinweis: "His message is equivalent with what we're trying to coach in our school ..." (Z. 36/37)

23. C
    Hinweis: "... Scary Guy's program was a success. 'I was astounded at the interest by our entire student body,' Earley says." (Z. 39/40)

24. A
    Hinweis: "... the middle school will make Scary Guy's message part of their teaching program." (Z. 48/49)

25. C
    Hinweis: "Scary Guy knows exactly how people are judging him, thinking he is ... a potentially dangerous person. All of this is based on the way he looks. But by the end of his presentation, they are lining up to give him hugs." (Z. 4–7)

Writing Part 1: International Work Camp

1. *Name:* eigener Name
   Age: eigenes Alter
   Sex: male/female
2. z. B. teaching children/helping people
3. z. B. German, English
   ✏ **Hinweis:** *Die Sprachen müssen großgeschrieben werden, sonst gibt es keinen Punkt.*
4. z. B. meeting friends/bungee jumping
5. z. B. Spain/France

Writing Part 2: Social Networks

Hi Gloria,

I know exactly what you mean. My boyfriend used to spend all evening chatting online, I'd say at least 5 hours a night. I like social networks as much as everyone else. It's great for finding out what my friends are up to and when there is a party etc. But my boyfriend spent all his free time online. So I got fed up and gave him an ultimatum: I told him he had to spend 3 hours every evening doing something with me instead of going online, or else I would leave him. So now we go out more often or we just stay home and play games. And both of us are much happier.
If your boyfriend would rather chat with strangers than spend time with you, you should find a boyfriend who really wants to be with you.

Good luck and best wishes,
(your name)

Writing Part 3: Two Tickets

✏ **Hinweis:** *Nur zwei der drei als Lösungsbeispiel gegebenen Aktivitäten müssen beschrieben werden.*

Hey Stephanie,
I've just got a super birthday present – two tickets for an event of my choice. And that's something that we could do together when you are here. Here are the two events I find most interesting.
The first activity is climbing. There is a climbing hall with climbing walls that are 7 to 12 metres high and with more than 200 different routes, both for beginners (like me) and more experienced people (like you). They also have a cafete-

ria, a sauna and a weight room, so if I don't get the hang of climbing, I can still entertain myself.
Alternatively, we could explore Berlin's underground on an official tour. We could see bunkers, transportation lines and many secret, forgotten places. It sounds really exciting and spooky! But if we decide to do that, you'd better bring a sweater, because it's always rather chilly underground!
A third option which might be interesting is to meet Batman. I know it sounds silly but I used to love him as a child and this multimedia event is said to be a new form of entertainment. It has special effects, acrobatics and stunts.
Which of the two would you like to go to? Tell me what you think.

Best wishes,
(your name)

Bildnachweis:
S. 2013-1: Fleisch © Thomas Perkins/Dreamstime.com; Würstchen © Vasiliy Koval/Dreamstime.com
S. 2013-3: Radio © PRILL Mediendesign/fotolia.de
S. 2013-4: Globe Theatre © Fotograf: Schlaier; http://commons.wikimedia.org/wiki/File:Globe_Theatre_London.jpg; public domain; Base Jumping © Fotograf: Xof711; http://en.wikipedia.org/wiki/File:03WAVRE006b.jpg; This file is licensed under the Creative Commons Attribution-Share Alike 3.0 Unported license.
S. 2013-10: Edinburgh Castle © Fotograf: Kim Traynor; http://en.wikipedia.org/wiki/File:Edinburgh_Castle_from_Portsburgh.jpg; This file is licensed under the Creative Commons Attribution-Share Alike 3.0 Unported license.
S. 2013-11: Royal Botanic Gardens © Fotograf: Steve nova; http://en.wikipedia.org/wiki/File:Palmhouse.jpg; This file is licensed under the Creative Commons Attribution-Share Alike 3.0 Unported license. Subject to disclaimers.; Royal Yacht Britannia © Fotograf: Akiramenai; http://en.wikipedia.org/wiki/File:HMY_Britannia.jpg; public domain.
S. 2013-17: Mädchen © Tamás Ambrits/Dreamstime.com
S. 2013-18: Kletterhalle © Andreas Resch/Dreamstime.com; Batman © picture alliance/empics

Schriftliche Prüfung zum MSA und zur eBBR in Berlin/Brandenburg
Englisch 2014

Listening Part 1: Recorded Messages

- You are going to hear two recorded messages.
- You will hear the recording twice.
- There are four questions in this part, two questions for each message.
- Look at the pictures and then listen to the recording.
- Choose the correct picture and put a tick (✓) in the right box.

Message One

1. On which day can you see "The Lion King" in the afternoon?

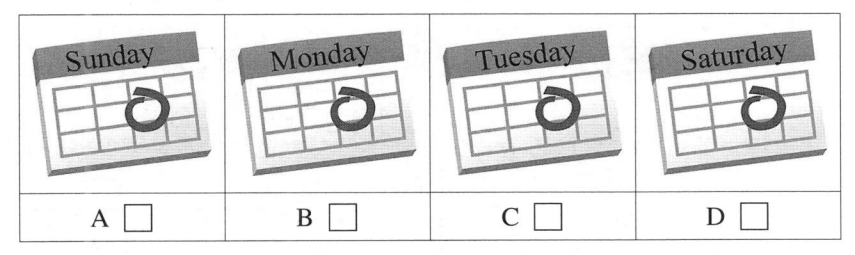

Sunday	Monday	Tuesday	Saturday
A ☐	B ☐	C ☐	D ☐

2. How much is the cheapest ticket for "The Lion King"?

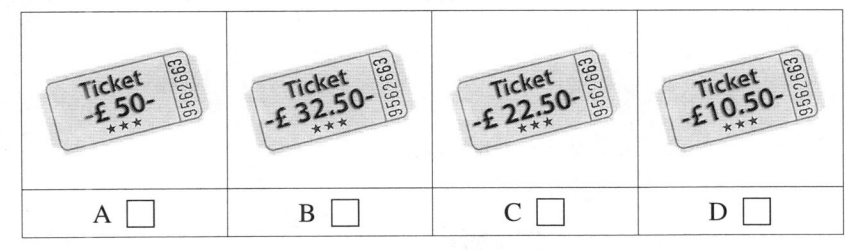

Ticket -£50-	Ticket -£32.50-	Ticket -£22.50-	Ticket -£10.50-
A ☐	B ☐	C ☐	D ☐

2014-1

Message Two

3. Which floor plan shows where the library is?

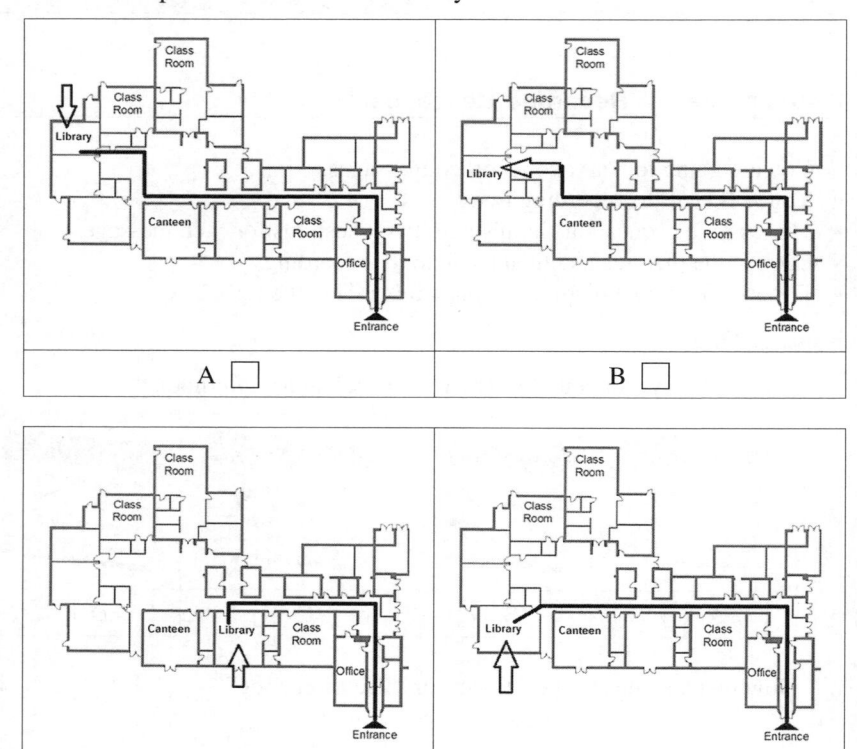

   A ☐   B ☐

   C ☐   D ☐

4. What should Carol bring to the library?

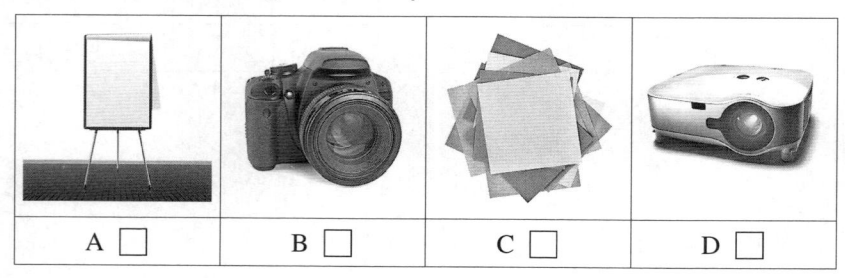

   A ☐   B ☐   C ☐   D ☐

Listening Part 2: Radio Ads

Please note: You do not need to understand every word to do this task.

- You are going to listen to four radio ads.
- You will hear the recording twice.
- Read the slogans below first, then listen to the recording.
- For each ad choose the correct slogan from the list (A–F) and put a tick (✓) in the right box.
- There is only one correct slogan for each ad.
- Two slogans can't be matched.

A   Don't be a fool – have breakfast at school.
B   Save the trees – collect old newspapers.
C   Keep your seat belt fastened.
D   Reading the newspaper will help you to get better marks.
E   Move your body – it's healthy and fun.
F   Buy from companies that don't experiment on animals.

	Radio Ads	Slogan					
		A	B	C	D	E	F
5.	Radio Ad 1						
6.	Radio Ad 2						
7.	Radio Ad 3						
8.	Radio Ad 4						

Listening Part 3: Unusual Hobbies

- You are going to hear three people talking about their unusual hobbies.
- You will hear the recording twice.
- Complete the table below using 1 to 5 words or numbers.

	What they do	Where they do it (Name one)	Why they do it (Name one)	People's reactions (Name one)
Cosplay	dress up in costumes	9.	10.	11.
Guerilla Gardening	secret gardening	12.	13.	14.
Extreme Ironing	combine ironing with extreme sport	15.	16.	17.

2014-4

✶ Listening Part 4: Dumpster Diving

- You are going to hear a radio show about Dumpster Diving.
- There are four people in the show: Sarah Parker (the presenter), Emily Dunne, Jeremy Williams and Alf Blake.
- You will hear the recording twice.
- Read the statements below first, then listen to the recording.
- Put a tick (✓) in the box next to the correct statement.
- Only one statement is correct in each case.

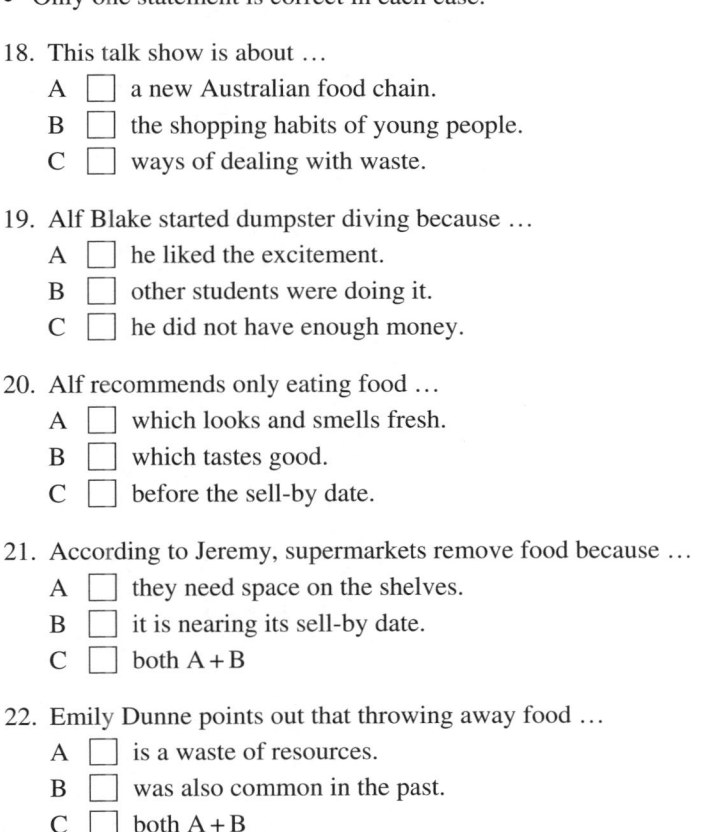

18. This talk show is about ...
    - A ☐ a new Australian food chain.
    - B ☐ the shopping habits of young people.
    - C ☐ ways of dealing with waste.

19. Alf Blake started dumpster diving because ...
    - A ☐ he liked the excitement.
    - B ☐ other students were doing it.
    - C ☐ he did not have enough money.

20. Alf recommends only eating food ...
    - A ☐ which looks and smells fresh.
    - B ☐ which tastes good.
    - C ☐ before the sell-by date.

21. According to Jeremy, supermarkets remove food because ...
    - A ☐ they need space on the shelves.
    - B ☐ it is nearing its sell-by date.
    - C ☐ both A + B

22. Emily Dunne points out that throwing away food ...
    - A ☐ is a waste of resources.
    - B ☐ was also common in the past.
    - C ☐ both A + B

23. Emily says that dumpster diving helps to ...
    A ☐ reduce environmental problems.
    B ☐ fight child labour in poor countries.
    C ☐ improve the quality of our food.

24. A lot of supermarket owners ...
    A ☐ offer cooking courses to their customers.
    B ☐ avoid throwing away their leftover food.
    C ☐ give money to the poor.

25. In Europe, dumpster divers are usually not arrested because ...
    A ☐ the legal situation is not clear.
    B ☐ the police have more serious problems to deal with.
    C ☐ both A + B

Listening: Candidate Answer Sheet   Name: _____

For students: Put a tick (✓) in the correct box.

Part 1: Recorded Messages

Number	A	B	C	D
1				
2				
3				
4				

/ 4 P

Part 2: Radio Ads

Number	Ads	Slogan					
		A	B	C	D	E	F
5	Radio Ad 1						
6	Radio Ad 2						
7	Radio Ad 3						
8	Radio Ad 4						

/ 4 P

Part 3: Unusual Hobbies

Die Ergebnisse müssen nicht übertragen werden.

/ 9 P

✶ Part 4: Dumpster Diving

Number	A	B	C
18			
19			
20			
21			
22			
23			
24			
25			

/ 8 P

/ 25 P

2014-7

Reading Part 1: Short Texts

- Look at the text and the statements in each task.
- What does the text say?
- Put a tick (✓) next to the statement that matches the text – **A, B, C** or **D**.
- There is only one correct statement for each sign.

1.

**Ymddiriedolaeth Genedlaethol
National Trust**

Do not pick our wild flowers
Please leave them for
every one to enjoy

This sign can be found:
A ☐ in a flower shop
B ☐ in a public park
C ☐ on a golf course
D ☐ in a private garden

2.

Abertawe Mwy Diogel
Safer Swansea

Dying to make that call? Switch off before you drive off!

A ☐ Don't drink and drive.
B ☐ Remember to turn off the lights.
C ☐ Don't use your phone while driving.
D ☐ Take a break when you are tired.

Quellennachweis: 2. © City and County of Swansea; 4. The Briarwood Clinic; 5. Matthew Young; 6. *Aus urheberrechtlichen Gründen musste der Originaltext der Prüfung abgeändert werden.

3.

THIS HOUSE IS MAINTAINED FOR THE COMFORT AND SECURITY OF MY DOGS. IF YOU CANNOT ACCEPT THAT THEN YOU CANNOT ACCEPT ME.

A ☐ The owner does not want dogs near the house.
B ☐ The owner's dogs are important for him/her.
C ☐ A security service monitors the house.
D ☐ Only visitors with dogs are allowed inside the house.

4.

PARENTS,
We appreciate you taking responsibility of your child while at The Briarwood Clinic.
Children left unattended will be given an espresso and a free puppy!

A ☐ Look after your children.
B ☐ Enjoy a free coffee.
C ☐ Here you can get a new toy for your child.
D ☐ In this hospital children get free medical help.

5.

Like the car? Don't let it leave without you. LOCK it!

A ☐ Make sure your car cannot be stolen.
B ☐ Buy your car from a used-car dealer.
C ☐ Don't forget to turn on your lights.
D ☐ Don't park your car on the street at night.

6.

After closing time, all the salads and sandwiches that weren't sold are handed out to food banks, which give them to poor and homeless people. This is not meant to be an act of "pity". Rather, we think that wasting wholesome food (and the work that went into producing it) would be crazy.*

The motto of this shop is:
A ☐ Don't throw leftover food away.
B ☐ Salad is good for you.
C ☐ Give money to the homeless.
D ☐ Keep the environment clean.

Reading Part 2: Internships

- These people (a–e) are looking for an internship.
- First read the information about the people, then look at the job offers (A–G) on the next page.
- In each case (a–e) find **two** jobs each person could apply for. Write the correct letters in the boxes next to the people's names.
- Some of the internships can be chosen more than once.

No.	Choice 1	Choice 2		Applicants
7/8				a) **Emma** (16) Emma is still at school and is looking for an internship during the summer holidays. She would like to do an internship in dressmaking and fashion since she loves sewing. She hopes she can combine this with a trip to America. If it doesn't work out, she can also imagine doing an internship in a restaurant. Personality: friendly; responsible; outgoing Likes: meeting new people; environmental projects Dislikes: office work; working on the computer
9/10				b) **Eun** (21) Eun is studying communication management. She would like to use her summer holidays to gain some work experience and if possible make some money at the same time. For her future career she would like to see how large events are organized. But she could also imagine finding an internship in which she can use her knowledge of visual digital media.

2014-10

11/12					Personality: friendly; good sense of humour Likes: travel; languages Dislikes: sports
				c)	**Dave** (16) Dave is a secondary school student. He would like to get a job in the hotel/restaurant business during the summer holidays because he has already gained some experience in this field. So he already knows how to deal with customers. On the other hand, he can also imagine working with kids because he loves playing with his younger brothers and sisters. Personality: lively; practical; outgoing Likes: sports; fitness; communicating; being outdoors Dislikes: working by himself/alone
13/14				d)	**James** (24) James is studying PE (physical education). He would like an internship in a sports centre where he can teach others or give classes preferably to adults. He would also consider working in an office environment as he thinks this experience would help him later if he decided to set up his own studio. If possible, he would like a job where he can take over some responsibility. Personality: confident; good sense of humour Likes: fashion; multitasking; sports; computers Dislikes: couch potatoes

15/16

e) **Mick** (16)
Mick doesn't know what he will do after finishing school. He would like to work with children who have special needs and would enjoy organizing trips for them. Alternatively, he would like to gain more experience in digital formatting. He has already created short clips for his friends' websites and helps them when they want to work on their digital photos.

Personality: friendly; reliable; outgoing
Likes: computers; sports; young children
Dislikes: office work

A) **Waiter/Waitress**

Host company profile: Hotel in Dublin City Centre
Responsibilities: Hosting and welcoming guests, serving food and beverages, collaborating with the manager, the kitchen and restaurant staff
Profile: Be dynamic and organized
Payment: Free meals
→ Four to six-week internships are possible between May and August.

B) **Assistant Coach**

Host company profile: Dublin Athletic Club. We coach and train disabled children up to the age of 12.
Responsibilities: To coach boys and girls with disabilities, help to set up programmes for fitness classes, help organize and carry out outdoor activities such as camping trips, help to clean and maintain the football pitch.
Profile: MUST love kids and sports, be less than 18 years of age and have excellent communication skills
Payment: None
→ The internship is immediately available and is full-time for 3 months.

C) Fitness Trainer

Host company profile: Dublin's finest health and fitness club
Responsibilities: Train and advise clients and help to organize fitness courses with the manager
Profile: Must be studying medicine or sports and have good communication and organization skills
Payment: Free monthly transport pass
→ The internship is immediately available (min 2–3 months).

D) Video Animation and Photography Assistant

Host company profile: This Dublin company provides Internet websites with images and movies.
Responsibilities: Editing and creating videos, assisting with photo retouch and correcting pictures responding to customer expectations
Profile: Must be creative, a good team player with a strong interest in multimedia and a good understanding of photography and video production
Payment: € 100 per week
→ The internship is available now for three months minimum.

E) Event Management Assistant

Host company profile: We deal with the general organisation of events. We are specialised in London and the UK but also coordinate festivals and tradeshows all over the world.
Responsibilities: Selling tickets, office administration, helping to set up an event
Profile: Must be a student in management, business or event and be between 21–25 years of age. Must have excellent use of spoken and written English and good use of standard computer applications
Payment: None. There is a huge possibility of interns becoming employees at our company.
→ The internship is immediately available and will last at least 4 weeks.

F) Front Desk Intern for Gochi Fashion

Host company profile: The leading fashion company, Gochi, is seeking a candidate for an office internship.
Responsibilities: Take incoming phone calls and perform data entry as needed. Do standard office work and be able to handle many different projects
Profile: Good use of standard computer applications, must be able to work independently, must have strong communication skills and be able to work under a deadline
Payment: None. There is a huge possibility of interns becoming employees at our company depending on the quality of work that they do for us.
→ The internship is immediately available and will last at least 4 weeks.

> G) **Fashion Design Internship Opportunity**
> **Host company profile:** A company in San Francisco, California that makes products out of recycled clothes
> **Responsibilities:** Designing new products e. g. bags, soft toys
> **Profile:** Have excellent communication skills, be able to complete tasks from start to finish, have a can-do attitude
> **Payment:** There is a huge possibility of interns becoming employees at our company.
> → The internship is immediately available and will last from June to August.

✶ Reading Part 3: Real-life Superheroes Patrol City Streets

- Read the text and the statements on the opposite page.
- Put a tick (✓) in the box next to the correct answer.
- Only one answer is correct in each case.

They patrol neighborhoods at night, but their identities are a secret. Many have full-time jobs and families. They're real-life superheroes who take the law into their own hands, just like comic book heroes. Your next-door neighbor could be one.

They're viewed as a welcome presence in communities where people need all the help they can get – or as reckless criminals who hinder police and put themselves and others at risk.

The latest additions to the group were three teens dressed as Batman and the Flash. The Royal Canadian Mounted Police warned the young superheroes – two are 17 and the third is 18 – for taking matters into their own hands. All three still live at home with their parents. By real-life superhero standards, they were amateurs, dressing as existing superheroes.

The hundreds of veterans have created their own personas. There's Thanatos in Vancouver, who's been patrolling the streets for four years dressed in a green- and-black mask, wide-brimmed hat and a black trench coat, handing out water, food and blankets to the city's homeless. In Iqaluit, a masked man known as Polarman has patrolled the streets for about a decade, keeping an eye out for vandals. And there's New York City's Dark Guardian – martial arts teacher Chris Pollak – whose specialty is creeping up to drug dealers in parks and yelling "This is a drug-free park!" while shining a light at them.

Michael Barnett, director of the documentary *Superheroes*, spent 17 months following and filming about 50 self-styled superheroes after discovering the movement online. Every "superhero" has their own story and these stories show that their motivations vary.

Some, like the Watchman, have a love of superheroes. The Wisconsin man puts on a mask to feed the homeless and has run successful toy drives for poor families during the holidays. He wouldn't talk about his day job, but said he has a wife and children and he's a college graduate. "I think the real world needs (superheroes) more than the comics and movies do, and I figured I can do my best to act like one," he said in an email, hiding his identity. "I was going to school to be a cop, but somewhere along the way I decided that wasn't what I wanted, yet I still wanted to do something."

"It's ultimately a protest movement. Instead of just protesting, they're actually trying to create change from the bottom up," Barnett said. "These are people who have no resources, for the most part, and they still are out there every night trying to do something. They're not any better off than some of the people they're trying to help, but they're still trying to help them."

But, few of the masked men and women out there actually fight crime – and they don't have superpowers. They mostly do community work, such as helping the homeless and patrolling troubled areas, handing out flyers.

Seattle's Phoenix Jones – real name Benjamin Fodor – leads the Rain City Superhero Movement, a group of self-styled superheroes who have patrolled the city since last year. Jones was arrested last month for using pepper spray to break up what he said was a fight outside a Seattle nightclub. No charges were filed, but the incident led to his dramatic unmasking as a father whose day job was working with autistic children. "Phoenix Jones is not a bad guy," said Edward Stinson, an author, who provides mentorship and advice to the real-life superheroes online. And he now stresses the fact that this is no longer a game.

As Seattle police spokesman Mark Jamieson said, intervening in potentially dangerous situations should be left to professional officers. "If people want to dress up and walk around, knock yourself out," he told the Associated Press. "Our concern is when you insert yourself into these situations without knowing the facts, it's just not a smart thing to do."

As the "heroes" continue to organize, Stinson said the eventual goal is to develop relationships with the local police. But Barnett doesn't think that's realistic. Superheroes like to do their own thing. "Most people are doing this because they don't like bureaucracy, they don't like rules," he said. "Police represent the system ... part of why they do this is they're rebelling against that."

Adapted from: Michael Woods: Real-life superheroes patrol city streets. In: The Star, Nov 27 2011.

17. Real-life superheroes …
    A ☐ are the stars of a new TV series.
    B ☐ want to be anonymous.
    C ☐ work for the police.
    D ☐ are former criminals.

18. The three teens who dressed up as superheroes …
    A ☐ had to undergo a test of courage.
    B ☐ were kicked out of their homes.
    C ☐ had problems with the police.
    D ☐ had some professional training.

19. Which of the following things done by a superhero is mentioned in the text (ll. 13–20)?
    A ☐ giving homeless people a place to sleep
    B ☐ trying to chase away drug dealers
    C ☐ removing illegal graffiti
    D ☐ all of them (A + B + C)

20. When Michael Barnett discovered the superhero movement, he …
    A ☐ made a documentary about it.
    B ☐ decided to write a book.
    C ☐ interviewed 17 superheroes.
    D ☐ became interested in joining it.

21. What information do we get about the Wisconsin man?
    A ☐ He comes from a poor family.
    B ☐ He has done charity work.
    C ☐ He works for the police.
    D ☐ both A + C

22. Barnett points out that the aim of these superheroes is …
    A ☐ to get public attention.
    B ☐ to make easy money.
    C ☐ to get help for their families.
    D ☐ to make the world a better place.

23. After Phoenix Jones was arrested, ...
    A ☐ he lost his job.
    B ☐ his true identity was revealed.
    C ☐ he was sent to a psychiatrist.
    D ☐ he started a self-help group.

24. Jamieson thinks that acting like a superhero is ...
    A ☐ risky.
    B ☐ foolish.
    C ☐ helpful.
    D ☐ both A + B

25. What could be the best alternative title for this article?
    A ☐ Beware of Superheroes!
    B ☐ From Superhero to Police Officer
    C ☐ Protect Your Neighborhood – Join the Superhero Movement!
    D ☐ Real-life Superheroes – How Super Are They Really?

Reading: Candidate Answer Sheet Name: _____

For students: Put a tick (✓) in the correct box.

Part 1: Short Texts

Number	A	B	C	D
1				
2				
3				
4				
5				
6				

/ 6 P

Part 2: Internships

Number	Name	A	B	C	D	E	F	G
7/8	a) Emma							
9/10	b) Eun							
11/12	c) Dave							
13/14	d) James							
15/16	e) Mick							

/ 10 P

✶ Part 3: Superheroes

Number	A	B	C	D
17				
18				
19				
20				
21				
22				
23				
24				
25				

/ 9 P

/ 25 P

Writing Part 1: How Green Are You?

- Complete the questionnaire below.
- Write keywords or short sentences.
- You may use your imagination.

How Green Are You?

Are you living a green life? Fill out the questionnaire and find out.

Age: ☐

Male: ☐   Female: ☐

(1) How do you get to school?

(2) What things do you recycle? (Name two)

(3) How do you save* electricity? (Name one)

(4) How do you save* water? (Name one)

(5) Which alternative energy do you think is most important?

SEND   HOME

* to save = *einsparen*

/ 5 P

Writing Part 2: Becoming a Vegetarian

- Read what the blogger has written.
- Then write back, answering all of his questions.
- Write 100–160 words.

| Home | Services | Blog | Contact | epinion |
| Welcome to our site | What we do | Read our stories | Get in touch | |

Blog ❯ Public topics ❯

Name: Meatie15   **Becoming a vegetarian**

My dad wants to stop eating meat and says that from now on he will only cook vegetarian dishes. But I can't live without my sausages, fried chicken, hamburgers … I'll die if all I get all day long are vegetables, vegetables and more vegetables! How about you and your family – what do you guys normally eat? I'd really like to know why people want to stop eating meat and become vegetarians. Any ideas? What do you think of vegetarians? I don't want my dad or me to argue about food all the time, so what can I do?

Inhalt: ___ / 6 P   Sprache: ___ / 6 P   Gesamt: ___ / 12 P

✱ Writing Part 3: Two Tickets

Große Hafenrundfahrt: das Tor zur Welt

Willkommen im Hamburger Hafen an Bord unserer schönen Schiffe, die vom Hamburger Hafen nicht mehr weg zu denken sind. Ahoi und hallo! Hier haben Sie Gelegenheit, den Hamburger Hafen mit all seinen Sehenswürdigkeiten in seiner Einmaligkeit und beeindruckenden Kontrasten zu besichtigen. Auf der Elbe und ihren Nebenarmen! Lassen Sie sich überraschen.

An Bord drinnen und draußen kann der Hafen in seiner ganzen Vielfalt und Weite bestaunt werden. Auf der Elbe gibt's nämlich jede Menge zu entdecken. Es geht vorbei am St. Pauli Fischmarkt, an den Docks und an riesigen Containerschiffen. Man sieht Ladekräne und Containerbrücken in Aktion, das gigantische Zelt, wo das Musical König der Löwen gespielt wird, die Hafencity, die halbfertige Elbphilharmonie und und und ...!

Abfahrt: St. Pauli Landungsbrücken, Br.3
Dauer: 1 ½ Stunden

Voca People Show

Auf professionelle Art macht VOCA PEOPLE nahezu jede Musik hörbar, und das ganz ohne Instrumente. Jenseits der Sonne gibt es einen uns bisher unbekannten, weißen Planeten Voca. Die lustigen Bewohner des Planeten leben seit etlichen Jahrtausenden friedlich miteinander und verständigen sich allein durch melodische Klänge.

An einem ganz besonderen Tag macht sich eine abenteuerlustige Gruppe auf den Weg, ihr Lebensmotto „Musik ist Leben und Leben ist Musik" in die Weiten des Universums zu tragen.

Doch auf ihrer intergalaktischen Musikreise sind sie zu einer Notlandung auf dem Planeten Erde gezwungen. Der Antrieb ihres Raumschiffs, der mit musikalischer Energie geladen wird, ist völlig entladen. Schnell wird ihnen bewusst, dass die menschliche Musik als perfekter Energielieferant für ihr Raumschiff dient.

Ort: CCH-Congress Center Hamburg Saal 2
Beginn: 20:00 Uhr

Eisdinner

In der Hansestadt erwartet Sie ein eisiges Ambiente, das eine besondere Ästhetik der Eiskunst gepaart mit kulinarischen Hochgenüssen verspricht.

Nachdem Sie mit einer warmen Daunenjacke eingekleidet worden sind, werden Sie in den kleinen Eispalast geführt. Hier erwartet Sie ein 2-Gang-Menü, das Ihnen im Eis kulinarisch einheizen wird. Genießen Sie die einzigartige Mischung aus eisigem Ambiente und warmen Köstlichkeiten.

In Ihrem Eis-Restaurant sind konstante −10°C. Auf 90 qm finden Sie eine Eistheke und beeindruckende Eis-Skulpturen. Faszinierende Farben werden durch Dioden-Illuminationen erzeugt und versprechen Ihnen ein einzigartiges Ambiente. Aufgrund der Temperatur ist ein Aufenthalt von länger als einer Stunde im Eis-Restaurant nicht möglich.

1. Adapted from: Kay Wiese, http://www.hafenrundfahrt-hamburg.com/
2. Adapted from: Semmel Concerts Veranstaltungsservice GmbH, Presseinformation Live in Concert 2014 Voca People
3. Adapted from: http://www.hamburg.de/dinner-shows/1572870/dinner-im-eis/

✶ Writing Part 3: Two Tickets

As a present for your birthday your parents want to give you two tickets for an event. You would like to go there with your Irish friend who you are going to meet in Hamburg.
- Read the three texts.
- Choose **two** events/activities.
- Write an e-mail to your friend telling him/her about the two events/activities you have chosen.
- For each one of them say what kind of event/activity it is and mention at least two more aspects that are important.
- **Do not translate word for word**, just give the main information used in these texts.
- Write complete sentences and use correct English.

To: friend@mail.com
Cc:
Subject: Hamburg

Hey _____ ,

I've just got a super birthday present – two tickets for an event of my choice. And that's something that we could do together when we meet in Hamburg. Here are the two things I find most interesting:

_____

_____

_____

_____

Which of the two would you like to go to? Tell me what you think.

☺ _____

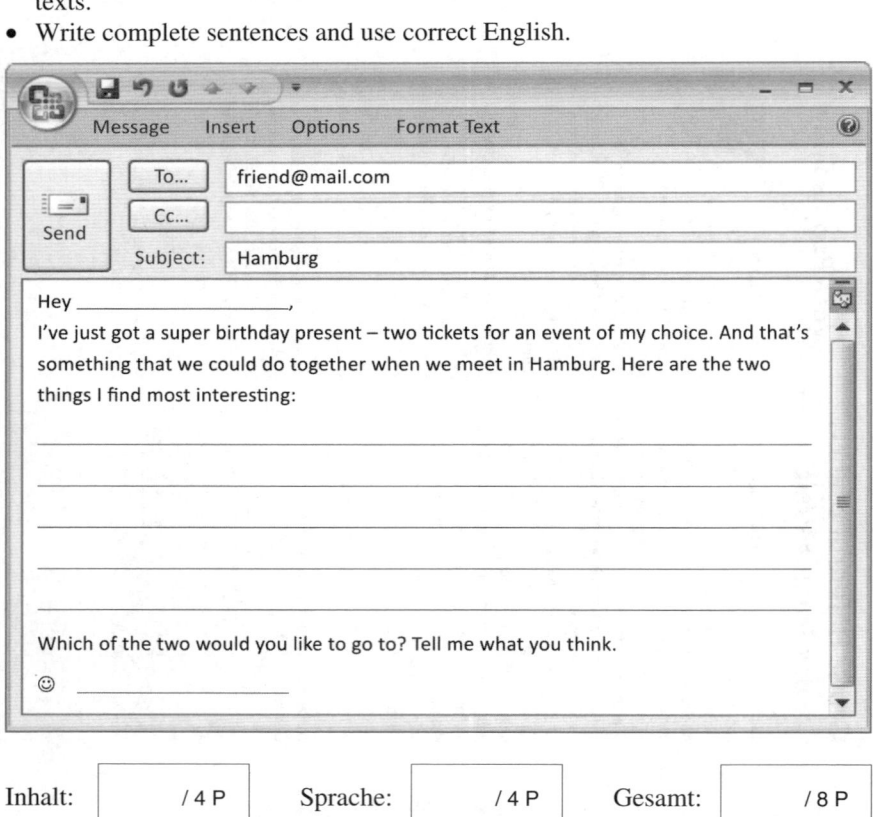

Inhalt: /4 P   Sprache: /4 P   Gesamt: /8 P

Lösungsvorschläge

Listening Part 1: Recorded Messages

Message One

1 Thank you for calling the Lyceum Theatre.
Show times for "The Lion King" are from Tuesday to Sunday at 7.30 pm with afternoon performances on Saturdays at 3 pm. There are no performances on Mondays.
5 The box office in Wellington Street is open between 10 am and 7 pm every day. Tickets for all performances are from £ 65 to £ 32 with student tickets for £ 22.50. We hope to welcome you soon at the Lyceum Theatre.

1. D
   Hinweis: "... afternoon performances on Saturdays at 3 pm." (Z. 3)
2. C
   Hinweis: "... student tickets for £ 22.50." (Z. 6)

Message Two

1 Hello Carol, where are you? We're waiting for you in the library. Just in case you've forgotten how to get here. When you enter the school building, walk straight on past the office. Then turn left and walk along the corridor to the end. The library is the last door on the left, next to the canteen.
5 I think we've got everything we need for our project. There is a projector and a flipchart in the library and Joanna has brought her camera. Hmm, wait a minute ..., I think we don't have enough coloured paper. On your way here, would you go to the office and ask Ms Anderson for some red and blue paper? Thanks. See you in a minute.

3. D
   Hinweis: "When you enter the school building, walk straight on past the office. Then turn left and walk along the corridor to the end. The library is the last door on the left, next to the canteen." (Z. 2–4)
4. C
   Hinweis: "... we don't have enough coloured paper ... would you ... ask Ms Anderson for some red and blue paper?" (Z. 7/8)

Listening Part 2: Radio Ads

Ad 1: Breakfast

A good breakfast at school means strong bodies and strong minds. Hello, I'm Agricultural Commissioner Todd Staples reminding you that your child's school has breakfast waiting for them every day. And you can be sure it's healthy and affordable. It's a fact that a nutritious start to the school day makes your child learn and perform better. Breakfast is a powerful thing. So power up with a healthy school breakfast every day. Sponsored by the US Department of Agriculture.

Todd Staples: School Breakfast – PSA (2/19/2009). © Texas Department of Agriculture

5. A

Hinweis: "A good breakfast at school means strong bodies and strong minds." (Z. 1); "... power up with a healthy school breakfast every day." (Z. 5/6)

Ad 2: Animal Testing

Some companies still test shampoos and household products on animals. 600 companies don't. For a free list showing which is which contact People for the Ethical Treatment of Animals, Norfolk, Virginia 23510. Thank you.

Courtesy of PETA, www.peta.org

6. F

Hinweis: "Some companies still test shampoos and household products on animals. 600 companies don't." (Z. 1/2)

Ad 3: Recycle

Hi, this is Sarah Nichols of the Indian River County Solid Waste Disposal District. Think about this: if everyone recycled all the copies of just one edition of the Sunday New York Times, we would save 75,000 trees. That's 75,000 trees. Think about all the trees we'd save if we recycled all the newspapers in the country. Most likely you do recycle but if you don't, give it a try. Special thanks to this station for allowing me to remind you to recycle.

http://www.ideagardenadvertising.com/psaaudio.htm [16. 01. 2013]

7. B

Hinweis: "... if everyone recycled all the copies of just one edition of the Sunday New York Times, we would save 75,000 trees." (Z. 2/3); "Think about all the trees we'd save if we recycled all the newspapers in the country." (Z. 4/5)

Ad 4: Turbulence

1 ANNCR: What a tough thing your body is. It's built to withstand bending ...
SFX: Exaggerated bending effect
ANNCR: Pinching ...
SFX: Ouch!
5 ANNCR: Tattooing ...
SFX: Sizzling sound
ANNCR: Swimming ...
SFX: Dunking noise
ANNCR: Bumping ...
10 SFX: Bonking effect
ANNCR: Tickling ...
SFX: Wild laughter
ANNCR: Shaving ...
SFX: Electric razor noise
15 ANNCR: Loud noises ...
SFX: Blaring music
ANNCR: Childbirth ...
SFX: Baby crying
ANNCR: Football ...
20 SFX: Tackling noise
ANNCR: Bad cooking ...
SFX: Sizzling/Alarm going off
ANNCR: Roller blading ...
SFX: Screeching noise
25 ANNCR: Marathons ...
SFX: Cheering crowd
ANNCR: Even company meetings ...
SFX: Snoring
ANNCR: But there's something the human body isn't built to withstand: unexpec-
30 ted turbulence. Happily, though, planes are built to withstand that, really well. All you have to do is wear your safety belt the entire flight. So next time you fly, stay buckled up. The whole time. Because after all, turbulence happens. And you're just not built for it.
TAG: This message is a public service of this station and the Federal Aviation
35 Administration.

Federal Aviation Administration: Turbulence 60 second PSA (July 10, 2013) © U.S. Department of Transportation

8. C

Hinweis: "All you have to do is wear your safety belt the entire flight. So next time you fly, stay buckled up." (Z. 31/32)

Listening Part 3: Unusual Hobbies

SPEAKER 1: Hi, I'm Josh and my unusual hobby is called Cosplay, which is short for "costume play". You see, Cosplayers like me get dressed up in a costume to look like your favourite actor or character from a movie or from a video game, a comic or even television. I'm crazy about Johnny Depp's Jack Sparrow and when people see me walking around the mall or down the street in the middle of town, I try to make them think I really am Jack Sparrow. I copy all of his typical movements and expressions, even his voice. I love to feel famous for a few hours. It's so funny to see how people react to me. Some of them stare, others just laugh. They probably think I'm promoting a film or something. And you know, there are even competitions and conventions where Cosplayers like me can meet and exchange experiences. It's great, you should try it!

SPEAKER 2: Hi there! My name is Samantha and my unusual hobby is called "guerrilla gardening". Gardening, you say? That doesn't sound unusual at all, more like work. But you see, what I do together with some friends is "secret gardening". We do it on empty city land, which is not used and looks really ugly, like those dirty places around trees, which are full of rubbish and dog poo. We get up in the middle of the night to secretly plant bushes and flowers. Even though this land is not used by anyone, what we guerrilla gardeners are doing is actually illegal and that makes the whole thing really exciting. You can be a rebel and do something good for your city at the same time! And you know, the next morning I watch people walk by and see them smile at what we have created! It's a wonderful feeling.

SPEAKER 3: I think what I do is the most unusual hobby of all. My name is Shaun and my hobby is called "extreme ironing". "What?" I hear you say. How can ironing be a hobby? Well, it's when you combine this boring household work with an extreme outdoor sport. I mean, imagine climbing a mountain with an ironing board on your back. When you've finally made it to the top, tired and out of breath, you're not finished yet. You've got to set up your board, take out your iron and start ironing your shirt. You see, extreme ironing gives you extra adrenalin and a well-pressed shirt as a bonus! And you can do this anywhere: in the middle of the desert or while riding your bike! Last summer I tried it out while I was kayaking with two friends. People sailing by thought we were crazy and maybe we are. But this hobby is different, it's extreme and it's great weekend fun!

9. mall (Z. 5)/in the street (Z. 5)/in town (Z. 6)/conventions (Z. 10)

10. love to feel famous (Z. 7/8)/funny to see reactions (Z. 8)

11. stare (Z. 9)/laugh (Z. 9)/think he promotes a film (Z. 9)/
    think he is Jack Sparrow/an actor (Z. 6)

12. on empty city land (Z. 16)/dirty places (around trees) (Z. 17)/land which
    looks ugly (Z. 16/17)/land which is not used (Z. 16)

13. illegal (Z. 20)/exciting (Z. 20/21)/be a rebel (Z. 21)/
    do something good (Z. 21)

14. smile (Z. 22)

15. outdoors (Z. 27)/mountain (Z. 27)/anywhere (Z. 31/32)/desert (Z. 32)/
    kayaking (Z. 33)

16. extra adrenalin (Z. 31)/extreme (Z. 34)/fun (Z. 35)/
    well-ironed shirt (Z. 31)/household work is boring (Z. 26)

17. think they are/he is crazy (Z. 34)
    Hinweis: Es gibt für diese Aufgabe keinen Punkt, wenn du nur das Wort *crazy* schreibst.

Listening Part 4: Dumpster Diving

1   SARAH: This is Sarah Parker from *TTR Radio*, and welcome to our weekly edition of *"Have Your Say"*! Ever heard about something called "Dumpster Diving"? You think it's some new kind of water sport? (*chuckle*) Far from it! A "dumpster" is the American word for the big metal rubbish bin that is
5   called a "skip" here in the UK and in Australia. And dumpster diving is actually looking for things in somebody else's rubbish. For example, dumpster divers eat the food and use the rubbish that other people throw away. Ewww! Doesn't that sound gross? And today you have the chance to find out more about dumpster diving from my guests here in the studio. First let me intro-
10 duce Emily Dunne, a documentary film-maker, who is interested in the consequences of the throw-away culture in Britain and America. Welcome, Emily.
    EMILY: Nice to be here.
    SARAH: Also here with us is Jeremy Williams, who owns a big supermarket in Bristol. Welcome Jeremy.
15 JEREMY: Hello.
    SARAH: And last but not least we have Alf Blake, a 26-year-old dumpster diver. Alf doesn't buy his food IN a supermarket, he takes what he wants out of the

big bins or dumpsters BEHIND the supermarket. He lives off the food and other things that are thrown away.

ALF: Hi.

SARAH: So Alf, tell us why you go dumpster diving.

ALF: Well I started dumpster diving or what I call dumpster DINING when I was a student simply because I couldn't afford to buy food – it was just too expensive. After finishing university I continued dumpster DINING because I didn't see the point in spending so much money on food when I can get it for free.

SARAH: But isn't it dangerous to eat old food that's been thrown away?

ALF: Well to start with, the food is hardly ever old. But, yes, eating food found in a dumpster can be risky. You always have to use good judgment. Use your nose and your eyes and your common sense. Be especially careful with eggs and meat. Wash everything really carefully when you get home. Don't worry too much about the sell-by dates. Supermarkets generally try to get rid of all foods nearing their sell-by date, because normally those foods just won't sell. Yet, a lot of products beyond the sell-by date are edible. In fact they taste great. And then often food gets thrown out because of the way it looks. This morning, for example, I had cereal that had been thrown away simply because the box was damaged, even though the inner plastic bag was OK.

SARAH: Now Jeremy, you have a supermarket. Is it true that supermarkets are throwing away perfectly good food?

JEREMY: Well in a way, yes. You know you have to get rid of food which doesn't look good, like bananas that have started to get brown spots. And of course sometimes food is taken from the shelf to make room for a new delivery. And as Alf has already mentioned we have to get rid of packaged food approaching its sell-by date. We try to offer our customers a great variety and everything should look nice and fresh for them. However, it …

ALF: You know, those bananas with the brown spots are perfect inside. There's no reason to throw them away.

SARAH: Emily, you dealt with this problem in your documentary film "Waste Not, Want Not".

EMILY: Yes, I did. And I think there's something very sad about the fact that we here in Britain are throwing out tons of food every year – especially when millions of people go to bed hungry. And not only supermarket owners are to blame. Restaurants and households also throw away tons of food every year. Wasting food is not only wasting money but is also really bad for the environment. When you throw out food, you're also throwing out the water and all of the resources, like the fuel and energy that were used to get that food to your plate. We really need to change things. We need to go back to the way our grandmothers bought and managed their food supplies.

SARAH: So you see Alf and other dumpster divers as environmentalists?

EMILY: Yes, definitely. In a way these guys are doing a great job. If not for them there would be even more waste in the big landfills outside the city. As we know food rotting in a landfill is really bad for our environment because of the methane gas it produces. And that methane is even more dangerous for our climate than the CO_2 coming out of cars. We have to stop wasting food. People also seem to forget that buying more than we need and throwing the rest away makes everything more expensive. So, more and more people can't afford to buy food. They then become dependent on waste to survive. In other words wasting food creates hunger and poverty.

JEREMY: Well, supermarkets do generate a lot of waste, but that doesn't mean it all ends up in the landfill. As I have already said, a supermarket owner has to remove food from the shelf but it doesn't all end up in a dumpster. We supermarket owners work together with composting companies. Every year tons of organic waste are composted or taken, for example, to pig farms. We also work with charity organizations. Last week, for instance, we donated bread, meat and vegetables to the Bristol soup kitchen, where the food was cooked and given to hungry families or individuals.

ALF: That's really nice to hear, Jeremy. I think you are one of the few. But believe me, there's still a lot of food being wasted.

EMILY: Definitely.

SARAH: Right. So, my final question before the break: Is dumpster diving actually legal?

ALF: Well, it depends. In the United States, for example, dumpster diving is generally legal, though on private property people can be arrested for burglary. This is unusual but a few years ago, two guys in Colorado got six months in prison after taking food from a grocer's private dumpster. In the United Kingdom and in Germany, taking items from a dumpster is viewed as theft but normally the police have so many other problems that they don't have time to crack down on us dumpster divers.

SARAH: Good for you. And it seems that we're hearing more and more about dumpster diving these days. So does that mean that dumpster diving is becoming socially acceptable? This is what we'll be talking about after the break. Stay tuned …

Based on: http://www.dumpstern.de/what-is-dumpster-diving/
http://www.clickclackgorilla.com/2011/01/27/legality-in-a-dumpster/
http://www.homelesshandbook.0catch.com/dining.html
http://www.feeding5k.org/food-waste-facts.php
http://welearntoday.com/skipping-the-new-way-of-food-shopping/
http://www.elephantjournal.com/2010/06/dumpster-diving-defeat-ban-on-turning-trash-into-treasure/ [20.08.2012]
http://en.wikipedia.org/wiki/Dumpster_diving [22.08.12]
http://www.ehow.com/facts_7148652_legality-dumpster-diving.html [22.08.2012]

18. C
   ▸ *Hinweis:* "... dumpster diving is actually looking for things in somebody else's rubbish ... dumpster divers eat the food and use the rubbish that other people throw away." (Z. 5–7)

19. C
   ▸ *Hinweis:* "Well I started dumpster diving ... simply because I couldn't afford to buy food – it was just too expensive." (Z. 22–24)

20. A
   ▸ *Hinweis:* "Use your nose and your eyes and your common sense." (Z. 29/30)

21. C
   ▸ *Hinweis:* "... sometimes food is taken from the shelf to make room for a new delivery ... we have to get rid of packaged food approaching its sell-by date." (Z. 42–44)

22. A
   ▸ *Hinweis:* "When you throw out food, you're also throwing out the water and all of the resources, like the fuel and energy that were used to get that food to your plate." (Z. 55–57)

23. A
   ▸ *Hinweis:* "... food rotting in a landfill is really bad for our environment ..." (Z. 62)

24. B
   ▸ *Hinweis:* "... a supermarket owner has to remove food from the shelf but it doesn't all end up in a dumpster. We supermarket owners work together with composting companies ... We also work with charity organizations." (Z. 70–74)

25. B
   ▸ *Hinweis:* "... normally the police have so many other problems that they don't have time to crack down on us dumpster divers." (Z. 86–88)

Reading Part 1: Short Texts

1. B
   ▸ *Hinweis:* "National Trust"; "wild flowers"; "for every one to enjoy"

2. C
   ▸ *Hinweis:* "... call"; "Switch off before you drive off!"

3. B
   Hinweis: "... for the comfort and security of my dogs."
4. A
   Hinweis: "We appreciate you taking responsibility of your child ..."
5. A
   Hinweis: "LOCK it!"
6. A
   Hinweis: "... we think that wasting wholesome food (and the work that went into producing it) would be crazy."

Reading Part 2: Internships

7./8. A, G
   Hinweis: Emma "... would like to do an internship in dressmaking and fashion ...", "... she can also imagine doing an internship in a restaurant."
   → job offer A: "Waiter/Waitress"
   → job offer G: "Fashion Design Internship Opportunity"
   Aufgrund der Überschrift "Front Desk Intern for Gochi Fashion" könnte man zunächst annehmen, dass Antwort F richtig sei. Es handelt sich aber um Büroarbeit am Computer, was Emma aber auf keinen Fall machen möchte ("Dislikes: office work, working on the computer").

9./10. D, E
   Hinweis: Eun "... would like to see how large events are organized.", "... use her knowledge of visual digital media."
   → job offer D: "Video Animation and Photography Assistant"
   → job offer E: "Event Management Assistant"

11./12. A, B
   Hinweis: Dave "... would like to get a job in the hotel/restaurant business ...", "... can also imagine working with kids ..."
   → job offer A: "Waiter/Waitress", "... Hotel in Dublin ..."
   → job offer B: "... coach and train disabled children ...",
   "MUST love kids and sports"; Dave "Likes: sports ..."

13./14. C, F
   Hinweis: James "... would like an internship in a sports centre ...", "... would also consider working in an office environment ..."
   → job offer C: "Fitness trainer"

Stellenangebot B scheidet aus, da James am liebsten mit Erwachsenen arbeiten möchte ("... preferably with adults ...").
→ *job offer F: "... office internship ..."*

15./16. B, D
✏ **Hinweis:** Mick "... would like to work with children who have special needs ...", "... would like to gain more experience in digital formatting."
→ *job offer B: "... coach boys and girls with disabilities ..."*
→ *job offer D: "... strong interest in multimedia ..."*

Reading Part 3: Real-life Superheroes Patrol City Streets

17. B
✏ **Hinweis:** "... their identities are a secret." (Z. 1)

18. C
✏ **Hinweis:** "The Royal Canadian Mounted Police warned the young superheroes ..." (Z. 9)

19. B
✏ **Hinweis:** "... creeping up to drug dealers in parks and yelling 'This is a drug-free park!'" (Z. 19/20)

20. A
✏ **Hinweis:** "Michael Barnett, director of the documentary *Superheroes* ..." (Z. 21)

21. B
✏ **Hinweis:** "The Wisconsin man puts on a mask to feed the homeless and has run successful toy drives for poor families ..." (Z. 25–27)

22. D
✏ **Hinweis:** "... they're actually trying to create change from the bottom up ..." (Z. 33/34), "... mostly do community work, such as helping the homeless and patrolling troubled areas ..." (Z. 39/40)

23. B
✏ **Hinweis:** "... led to his dramatic unmasking as a father whose day job was working with autistic children." (Z. 45/46)

24. D
✏ **Hinweis:** "... intervening in potentially dangerous situations ..." (Z. 49/50), "... when you insert yourself into these situations without knowing the facts, it's just not a smart thing to do." (Z. 52/53)

25. D

Hinweis: Der Artikel warnt weder einseitig vor den Risiken durch selbsternannte Superhelden (Überschrift A), noch macht er unverhohlen Werbung für die Superheldenbewegung (Überschrift C), noch rückt er eine einzelne Person besonders in den Vordergrund (Überschrift B). Es geht vielmehr um eine möglichst ausgewogene Darstellung (Pro und Kontra) eines neuartigen Phänomens – Überschrift D ist daher als Alternativtitel am besten geeignet.

Writing Part 1: How Green Are You?

Age: eigenes Alter
Sex: male/female

1. z. B. I get to school by bike.
2. z. B. I recycle paper and plastic.
3. z. B. I use energy-saving light bulbs or LED only.
4. z. B. I stop the toilet from flushing too long.
5. z. B. I think solar energy is most important.

Writing Part 2: Becoming a Vegetarian

Hinweis: Achte darauf, in deiner Antwort wirklich auf alle Fragen des Bloggers einzugehen. Du musst also kurz die Essgewohnheiten deiner Familie skizzieren, mögliche Gründe für eine vegetarische Ernährung nennen, deine eigene Meinung zu Vegetariern darstellen und einen Vorschlag machen, wie Meatie15 am besten mit der geschilderten Situation umgehen soll. Versuche trotzdem, dich innerhalb der geforderten Wortzahl zu bewegen. Die untenstehende Beispiellösung ist nur eine von vielen Möglichkeiten, diese Aufgabe zu bearbeiten.

Hi Meatie15,

My family eats all kinds of food – a little bit of meat and fish, but also lots of rice, pasta, fruit and vegetables.

Our neighbour is a vegetarian and she has stopped eating meat because the animals raised for food are not treated well. They are kept in small cages and don't have room to move, and that's why they get ill easily and are given antibiotics. My neighbour also says that a vegetarian diet is healthier, because you don't eat so much fat.

I think being a vegetarian is cool and it seems healthier, though I do like eating steak or fish now and then.

Why don't you and your dad cook together? Your dad can make the vegetarian dishes and you can make some sausages or meat to have as well. Otherwise if your dad doesn't want meat in the house, you might just eat your sausages when you're in the school cafeteria.

Best wishes,

(your name) (159 words)

Writing Part 3: Two Tickets

🖋 **Hinweis:** *Zur besseren Veranschaulichung wurden in der folgenden Beispiellösung alle drei angegebenen Aktivitäten bzw. Veranstaltungen kurz skizziert – in deiner Lösung musst du allerdings nur zwei davon beschreiben.*

Hey Sean,

I've just got a super birthday present – two tickets for an event of my choice. And that's something that we could do together when we meet in Hamburg. Here are the two things I find most interesting:

Taking a tour of the Hamburg harbour would be great. The boat sails on the Elbe as well as some side rivers. We'll be able to see huge container ships, go past the famous St. Pauli fish market and see the docks where the ships are repaired.

Then, there's a funny performance by a group of singers called the *Voca People*. They say they're from another planet so it should be interesting. They only communicate by melodic sounds and have landed here on Earth due to an emergency while travelling through space. They have to recharge their spaceship with musical energy and that's where the performance comes in.

Finally, we could go out for dinner to a literally "cool" location – an ice restaurant. As the room temperature there is minus 10 degrees, all the customers are clothed in warm down jackets before they are served a two-course menu among beautifully illuminated ice sculptures.

Which of the two would you like to go to? Tell me what you think.

☺ Yours, *(your name)* (153 words)

Schriftliche Prüfung zum MSA und zur eBBR in Berlin/Brandenburg
Englisch 2015

Listening Part 1: Short Messages

- You are going to hear two short messages.
- You will hear the recording twice.
- There are four questions in this part, two questions for each message.
- Look at the pictures and then listen to the recording.
- Choose the correct picture and put a tick (✓) in the right box.

Message One

1. What is Taylor's shoe size?

   A ☐   B ☐   C ☐   D ☐

2. What does Taylor need the shoes for?

   A ☐   B ☐

2015-1

| C ☐ | D ☐ |

Message Two

3. Which room can you book at Blueberry Lodge?

Room 8	Room 9
A ☐	B ☐

Room 10	Room 11
C ☐	D ☐

4. Which service do you have to pay for at Blueberry Lodge?

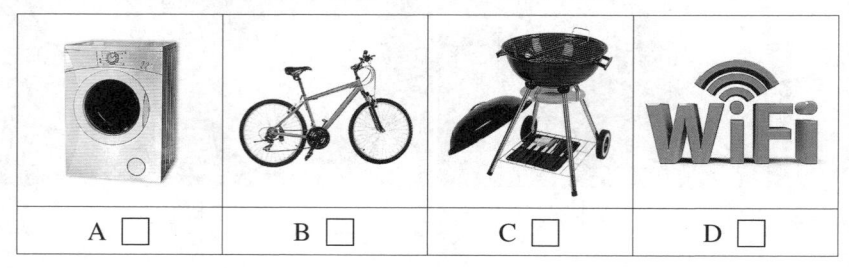

| A ☐ | B ☐ | C ☐ | D ☐ |

Listening Part 2: Radio Ads

Please note: You do not need to understand every word to do this task.

- You are going to listen to four radio ads.
- You will hear the recording twice.
- Read the slogans below first, then listen to the recording.
- For each ad choose the correct slogan from the list (A–F) and put a tick (✓) in the right box.
- There is only one correct slogan for each ad.
- Two slogans can't be matched.

A Sign up for one of our courses.
B Support your child's school career.
C Always keep fires under control.
D Be sure to drink enough water.
E Go camping with your children.
F Keep the environment clean.

	Radio Ads	Slogan					
		A	B	C	D	E	F
5.	Radio Ad 1						
6.	Radio Ad 2						
7.	Radio Ad 3						
8.	Radio Ad 4						

Listening Part 3: World Alternative Games

- You are going to hear descriptions of three unusual sports.
- You will hear the recording twice.
- Complete the table below using 1 to 5 words or numbers.

	Where from?	What to wear? (Name one)	How far?	Which rules? (Name one)
Stiletto Racing	*nobody knows*	9.	10. _____ metres	11.
Wife Carrying	12.	13.	14. _____ metres	*same-sex couples allowed*
Egg Throwing	15.	16.		17.

2015-4

✶ Listening Part 4: Fast Fashion

- You are going to hear a radio show.
- There are four people in the show: Talma Williams (the presenter), Malvin Kureishi, Hannah Flynn and Bill Wallace.
- You will hear the recording twice.
- Read the statements below first, then listen to the recording.
- Put a tick (✓) in the box next to the correct statement.
- Only one statement is correct in each case.

18. The guest Hannah ...
    A ☐ is a dressmaker.
    B ☐ has written a book on fashion.
    C ☐ owns a clothes shop.

19. Malvin goes clothes shopping ...
    A ☐ every week.
    B ☐ on the Internet.
    C ☐ both A + B

20. Why do people post haul videos according to Malvin?
    A ☐ to show what they've bought
    B ☐ to give styling tips
    C ☐ both A + B

21. Bill has become successful because ...
    A ☐ his website attracts a lot of customers.
    B ☐ he works longer hours than other businessmen.
    C ☐ he changes the clothes in his shops more often than others.

22. Hannah points out that fast fashion clothes ...
    A ☐ are produced by unfairly treated workers.
    B ☐ should be sold at a lower price.
    C ☐ are made of low-quality material.

2015-5

23. What does Bill mean by the "democratisation of luxury"?
    A ☐ Old clothes are passed on to others.
    B ☐ Everybody can wear the latest designs.
    C ☐ Ordinary people present his clothes on the catwalk.

24. According to Hannah, shoppers should …
    A ☐ know more about how clothes are produced.
    B ☐ think about their shopping habits.
    C ☐ both A + B

25. A possible alternative title for this talk show could be …
    A ☐ The Price of Fashion
    B ☐ A Shoppers' Paradise
    C ☐ The Future of Shopping

Listening: Candidate Answer Sheet   Name: _____

For students: Put a tick (✓) in the correct box.

Part 1: Short Messages

Number	A	B	C	D
1				
2				
3				
4				

/ 4 P

Part 2: Radio Ads

Number	Ads	Slogan					
		A	B	C	D	E	F
5	Radio Ad 1						
6	Radio Ad 2						
7	Radio Ad 3						
8	Radio Ad 4						

/ 4 P

Part 3: World Alternative Games

Die Ergebnisse müssen nicht übertragen werden.

/ 9 P

★ Part 4: Fast Fashion

Number	A	B	C
18			
19			
20			
21			
22			
23			
24			
25			

/ 8 P

/ 25 P

Reading Part 1: Watching TV

- These people (a–e) want to watch some TV.
- First read the information about the people, then look at the descriptions of the programmes (A–G) on pages 10 and 11.
- In each case (a–e) find the **two** programmes each person would watch. Write the letters of the programmes in the boxes next to the viewers' names.
- Some of the programmes can be chosen more than once.

No.	Pro 1	Pro 2	The viewers
1/2	B	C	a) **Raju** (40) a construction worker from Pakistan who lives in Great Britain, misses his home country and the Pakistani culture very much. He likes watching funny series about immigrant families. Alternatively, he likes to watch programmes that have something to do with his job.
3/4	E	F	b) **Sami** (17) is working on a presentation about the situation of homosexuals in different countries and is looking for a helpful programme on TV. In his free time he works as a dog-sitter and is naturally interested in finding out as much as possible about these furry friends.
5/6	F	C	c) **Grace** (60) lives together with her husband John. Since her husband once worked for a big construction company, they like to watch programmes with some heavy construction going on. When she is alone, she enjoys touching stories about pets and their owners.

2015-8

7/8	B	D		d) **Imogen** (16) loves animals and is especially interested in helping endangered ones. She tries to watch programmes that give her an idea of what she can do to help. She is also a humorous person who enjoys watching comedies with lots of good jokes.
9/10	G	A		e) **Shaniqua** (19) shows great interest in landscape photography. At weekends she likes travelling to the countryside to take pictures. She is also interested in programmes that she can relate to, for example the situation at home – her older brother doesn't want to move out of his comfort zone.

A) The Great British Year

Spring is the start of a race for life where timing is everything; trees explode with blossom and mornings fill with the magical chorus of bird song. Birds frantically build nests, while in our oceans seahorses court each other as if dancing elegantly. As we celebrate Easter, a stoat mother hunts the young rabbits to feed her own playful young. As spring becomes summer, Guillemot chicks leap from their cliffs to begin life at sea, and this year's young prepare for life alone.

This documentary about spring in Britain is packed with beautiful photography.

B) Citizen Khan

The second series of the family sitcom about the British-Pakistani Khans and their unlucky, busybody head of the family (played by Adil Ray), which is set in the capital of British Pakistan – Sparkhill, Birmingham, kicks off with the discovery that daughter Alia has failed her exams. Mrs Khan desperately wants her to go to college – but when Mr Khan learns how much it'll cost, he looks for a cheaper option. You will laugh yourself sick.

C) The Crane Gang

Enter the world of the 'heavies' – the team behind the huge machines that are challenged with carrying out the biggest lifts of all. The pressure is on as the UK's largest mobile crane company has to lift a very expensive sculpture into a private home in Somerset. Meanwhile in east London, the removal of an old railway bridge turns into a big problem. For crane driver teams like Leigh and Lee, it all means a hard and often frustrating 24/7 schedule.

D) Britain's Big Wildlife Revival

The series returns to walk through our wetlands in search of wildlife. Many animals are in danger because of alien invaders, or as a result of our tidying up and building on the countryside. So now, the discovery of a rare species on a building site can stop work completely.

Many animals living in our wetlands aren't pretty, but they play an important part in keeping the balance of our environment. Mike Dilger shows how you can help, too, by building a garden pond, even a tiny one made from a dustbin lid.

E) Stephen Fry, Out There

This episode sees Stephen visit Brazil, home to the largest gay pride celebration in the world and a place that has some of the best legislation on the planet for gay equality. But it has come at a price. All of the advances have brought about violence against gay people; on average, one gay person is murdered every 36 hours in Brazil. Stephen sees how this influences the lives of gay men and women there and also confronts the politician leading the fight against gay rights.

F) The Wonder of Dogs

This time the team looks at the special relationship between people and dogs. How much of our pets' behaviour and personality is as a result of their nature and how much comes from us? They discover how dogs have developed to understand us better than any other creature on the planet, even better than our closest living relative, the chimpanzee. Ruth Goodman looks deep into the history of Greyfriars Bobby, one of the most famous dogs in the world. This loyal dog guarded his master's grave for 14 years.

G) Hotel of Mum and Dad

We meet sci-fi fanatics Ellie Rose and Mitch from Norwich. Mummy's boy Mitch is refusing to grow up. He is used to his mum doing every little thing for him and this is driving his girlfriend Ellie mad. She desperately wants Mitch to move out and she wants them to get a place of their own. But there's one problem – his mum just doesn't want to let him go. Can Ellie finally persuade Mitch to get a job and start earning so they can stand on their own two feet and get their own place? Or will this mummy's boy be running home at the end of the week?

Quellennachweis:
Text A (The Great British Year): BBC One, http://bbc.co.uk/programmes/p01dfksf
Text C (The Crane Gang): BBC Two, http://bbc.co.uk/programmes/b03bmg9n
Text E (Stephen Fry, Out There): BBC Two, http://bbc.co.uk/programmes/b03dyv3k
Text F (The Wonder of Dogs): BBC Two, http://bbc.co.uk/programmes/b03c7j45
Text G (Hotel of Mum and Dad): BBC Three, http://bbc.co.uk/programmes/b03d5kqh

Reading Part 2: Short Texts

- Look at the text and the statements in each task.
- Put a tick (✓) next to the statement that matches the text – **A**, **B**, **C** or **D**.
- There is only one correct statement for each sign.

11. **RSC** Royal Shakespeare Company

Please ensure that this door is closed behind you and that you do not hold the door open for anyone who does not have a tower ticket.

To open the door, please press the small silver button below and NOT the green emergency release pad.

Many thanks

A ☐ Press the green button to open the door.
B ☐ Be polite – open the door for other guests.
C ☐ This door may only be used in an emergency.
D ☒ You may only enter if you have a ticket.

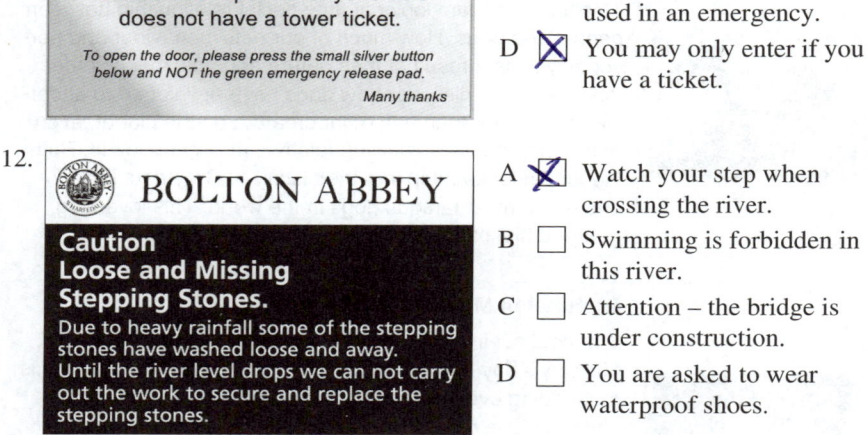

12. **BOLTON ABBEY**

Caution
Loose and Missing Stepping Stones.
Due to heavy rainfall some of the stepping stones have washed loose and away. Until the river level drops we can not carry out the work to secure and replace the stepping stones.

A ☒ Watch your step when crossing the river.
B ☐ Swimming is forbidden in this river.
C ☐ Attention – the bridge is under construction.
D ☐ You are asked to wear waterproof shoes.

13.

MAGDALEN BRIDGE BOATHOUSE

SAFETY NOTICE

Non swimmers should not pole boats.
Life jackets are available upon request.
Red cushions are buoyancy cushions.

SURCHARGES

Boats returned in a flooded condition charged at. £5
Overloaded boats will be charged double. HOUR REG RATE
Boats pulled off river and overturned charged at. £10
Boats returned after closing time charged at every 15 minutes. £20

Loss and damage will be charged for.

PLEASE RESPECT THE BOATS

A ☐ You must clean the boat before returning it.
B ☐ You can't return your boat after the boathouse closes.
C ☒ Handle the boats with care.
D ☐ Pay for the boat before renting it.

14.

The more you LEARN
The more you EARN

Almost overnight, DeAndre's shoe size jumped from 12 to 15. He decided – right then and there – to design shoes for other guys with big feet. It wouldn't be easy. He wasn't doing well in school – even got expelled. But DeAndre finally decided that enough was enough, and he needed to change. He started going to school every day, getting to class on time and turning in his assignments. His hard work paid off; he is getting A's and is headed for college.
In a few years, check for **"Shoes by DeAndre"** in stores across the country.

As DeAndre wanted to start his own business, he

A ☐ needed a new outfit.
B ☒ began working hard at school.
C ☐ worked part-time in a shoe store.
D ☐ quit school at the age of 15.

15.

Video cameras

For your added security video cameras are being introduced on London Underground trains

People who assault our staff or vandalise our property will be prosecuted

A ☒ Video cameras will improve safety on the Underground.

B ☐ An action film is being shot in this underground station – do not disturb.

C ☐ You are not allowed to use your video camera on the Underground.

D ☐ More staff will help you find your way on the Underground system.

16.

If you are ever trapped under a ton of rubble, I promise to sniff you out.

I promise to be worth every cent of the $ 10,000 that it took to train me.
I promise to ignore all other more fascinating smells and concentrate on the scent of live humans.
I promise to go about my work with a wagging tail, even if my paws get sore.
I promise to never give up.

National Disaster Search Dog Foundation
Strengthening disaster response in America by teaming the most highly trained dogs with firefighters to save lives.

To donate, call (888) 459-4376 or visit www.searchdogfoundation.org.
http://www.bloomingdaleanimalhospital.com/national-disaster-search-dog-foundation.html

A ☒ Support the training of dogs that find people in danger.

B ☐ Train your dog to make your life more fun.

C ☐ Save a dog's life – give it a good home.

D ☐ In case of a disaster, don't leave your dog behind.

Quellennachweis:
14. © Campbell & Company Communications; 16. © Photographer Deborah Samuels who donated her creative photo. Young & Rubicam, New York – Marketing and Communication Firm.

★ Reading Part 3: Educating Yorkshire

- Read the text and the statements on pages 17 and 18.
- Put a tick (✓) in the box next to the correct answer.
- Only one answer is correct in each case.

Georgia is a 16-year-old with a lousy attitude; she swears at the teachers, won't wear her school uniform and storms out of class when she's told off. But the platinum blonde is also the first of her family to almost reach the end of her school life without being kicked out, and her teachers at the Thornhill Community Academy are proud that she is going to take her GCSEs[1].

Georgia is one of the 'stars' of Educating Yorkshire. By turns horrifying and heartwarming, this reality TV show makes fascinating viewing even if it is, at times, a little uncomfortable. Filmed over eight weeks, it shows life at the comprehensive school in Dewsbury, Yorkshire, from teachers' meetings in the staff room to pupils dancing at the school prom. Each story is interesting and exciting, from the young Asian girl working really hard for her GCSEs, to the bullied boy who can't stop punching others.

At the heart of it all is head teacher Jonny Mitchell, who really likes singing to himself. He's been at Thornhill for just under two years and he's determined to give his pupils a decent education and teach them how to be model citizens; even if it's the last thing they want.

'Dewsbury, to most people, has negative connotations,' says Jonny, 'but we wanted to do something to make our young children proud. We're trying very hard to make their lives better under difficult circumstances.' Dewsbury has a 20 per cent unemployment rate and Jonny estimates that 10 per cent of his pupils' parents work in offices; the rest are industrial workers or are unemployed. Half his students are of Asian, mainly Pakistani, origin while the rest are white British.

Thornhill, a former failing school, is now rated 'good' in school inspections. It was expected to get 45 per cent A–C grades at GCSE last year but it actually managed 63 per cent.

'I think we're doing a fantastic job and I wanted to put that across,' says Jonny of his reasons for agreeing to 65 cameras being placed in almost every corner of his school. 'I think our kids are brilliant and they deserve to experience something a little bit different.' Jonny says staff and pupils were only really aware of the cameras for the first few days. In the first 20 minutes the kids did not show any respect. Instead they were showing off, making all sorts of faces and gestures. 'We told them you won't be a TV star if you make all these obscene gestures and they stopped. For the first two days it felt weird, but quite exciting. Everyone was coming in with new hairdos. But then it was business as usual although, generally, behaviour improved a bit. It's still better than it was; I think that's because they know the show's coming out.'

The programme certainly shows the ups and downs of teaching. There are huge challenges, from the children whose behaviour constantly disrupts classes to the boy with a stutter who's terrified about how he'll cope with his oral examinations.

There are also embarrassing and tragic moments, such as when Jonny has to tell a boy's shocked mother that he hasn't behaved well enough to go to the school prom. She'd already taken out a loan of £1,500 to hire a sports car and £2,000 on a suit for her son. 'The prom thing is ridiculous, it's quite obscene,' says Jonny. 'A lot of our families are financially deprived but they all want to keep up with each other. They spend shedloads on a dress their daughters will never wear again. It's bonkers.'

Over 100 schools volunteered to be featured, and it took ten months for Thornhill to be chosen and for its staff, pupils and parents to get to know the producers and be fully on board. It was quite a risk for the headmaster and his colleagues to trust the two producers whom they had only known for a few months. The whole project could have turned out to be a disaster for the school's reputation. But the risk was worth taking.

Although consent forms had to be signed at every stage of the process, the school had no editorial control and sometimes the teachers as well as the pupils are seen making mistakes. 'It shows humanity,' says Jonny. 'Yes it shows error, but it also shows people working hard. I don't think any of us come out of it at all badly.'

Jonny, who looks like a nightclub bouncer but actually began his working life as an accountant, is hoping the show will attract more pupils to his school.

Educating Yorkshire, Thursday, 9 pm, Channel 4.

Adapted from: Joe Brockman, Daily Mail 30 Aug 2013.

1 GCSE: General Certificate of Secondary Education; a British exam taken by students usually around the age of 16.

17. Georgia, one of the stars in the reality show, ...
    A ☐ behaves badly at school.
    B ☐ wants to be a hairdresser.
    C ☐ will take an exam.
    D ☐ both A + C

18. *Educating Yorkshire* shows scenes ...
    A ☐ in the teachers' room.
    B ☐ from a dance event.
    C ☐ with a student studying for an exam.
    D ☐ all of them (A + B + C)

19. The students at this school ...
    A ☐ mostly come from rich families.
    B ☐ are all immigrants from different countries.
    C ☐ managed to get better test results than before.
    D ☐ both A + B

20. When the filming began, the students did not ...
    A ☐ want to be filmed.
    B ☐ do any homework.
    C ☐ come to school.
    D ☐ behave well.

21. One effect of the show is that ...
    A ☐ the teachers work together more.
    B ☐ the school has won a prize.
    C ☐ the students behave better.
    D ☐ the parents support the teachers more.

22. What does Jonny think about the prom?
    A ☐ Students should be better prepared for it.
    B ☐ Parents spend too much money on it.
    C ☐ It is difficult to organise.
    D ☐ all of them (A + B + C)

23. The show was filmed at Thornhill because …
    A ☐ the producers were interested in bullying at school.
    B ☐ the school wanted to take part and was accepted.
    C ☐ the headmaster and the producer were old friends.
    D ☐ the parents wanted to make the school's problems public.

24. According to Jonny, …
    A ☐ the show gives an unrealistic picture of school life.
    B ☐ the producers should have had more influence.
    C ☐ the show illustrates that making mistakes is human.
    D ☐ the producers had problems with the parents.

25. What could be the best alternative title for this article?
    A ☐ Be a Headmaster – Become a Star
    B ☐ Media Education Today
    C ☐ Tough Teachers at Work
    D ☐ Reality TV Meets Real School Life

Reading: Candidate Answer Sheet   Name: _____

For students: Put a tick (✓) in the correct box.

Part 1: Watching TV

Number	Name	A	B	C	D	E	F	G
1/2	a) Raju							
3/4	b) Sami							
5/6	c) Grace							
7/8	d) Imogen							
9/10	e) Shaniqua							

/ 10 P

Part 2: Short Texts

Number	A	B	C	D
11				
12				
13				
14				
15				
16				

/ 6 P

✶ Part 3: Educating Yorkshire

Number	A	B	C	D
17				
18				
19				
20				
21				
22				
23				
24				
25				

/ 9 P

/ 25 P

Writing Part 1: A New Soap* Character

- Complete the questionnaire below.
- Write keywords or short sentences.

Meet the Johnsons

Channel 5 would like to create a new soap opera called "Meet the Johnsons". You can help by creating a character profile. Please fill out the questionnaire.

Name of character

Age

Male   Female

(1) What job does your character have?

(2) What hobbies does your character have? (Name two)

(3) Name one positive and one negative quality of your character.

(4) Name something special your character has done.

(5) What does your character want to do in the future?

SEND   HOME

* soap (= soap opera): A TV series about the lives and problems of a group of people

/ 5 P

Writing Part 2: Mobile Phones

- Read what a blogger has written below.
- Then write back, answering all of his questions.
- Write 100–160 words.

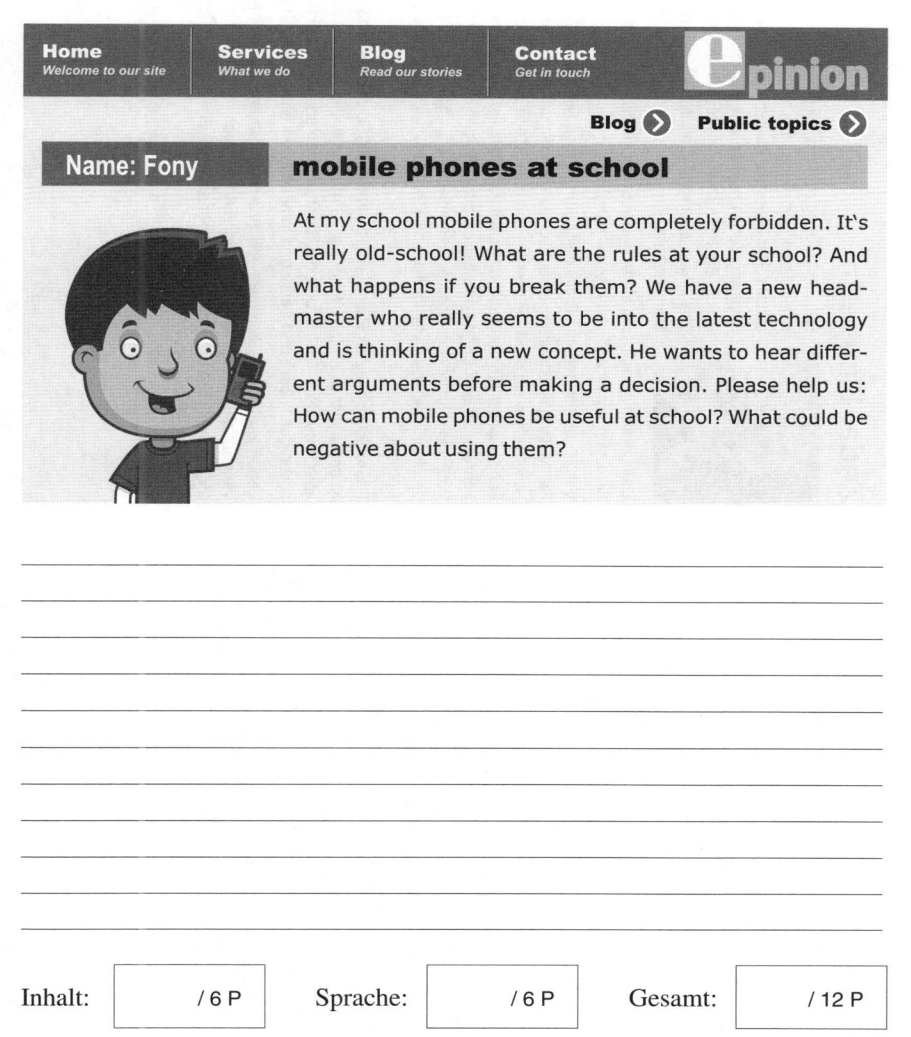

Home — Welcome to our site
Services — What we do
Blog — Read our stories
Contact — Get in touch

epinion

Blog ▶   Public topics ▶

Name: Fony

mobile phones at school

At my school mobile phones are completely forbidden. It's really old-school! What are the rules at your school? And what happens if you break them? We have a new headmaster who really seems to be into the latest technology and is thinking of a new concept. He wants to hear different arguments before making a decision. Please help us: How can mobile phones be useful at school? What could be negative about using them?

Inhalt: ___ / 6 P   Sprache: ___ / 6 P   Gesamt: ___ / 12 P

✶ Writing Part 3: Mediation – Young Careers

Lukas Mielke:
Deutschlands jüngster Unternehmer

Er ist gerade erst volljährig und hat schon 40 Mitarbeiter. Lukas Mielke, ein junger Berliner Unternehmer. Lukas Mielke spricht kaum einen Satz zu Ende. Mal klingelt das Handy, mal platzt ein Kollege ins Büro. Alle wollen etwas von Mielke.

Wie viel Geld Mielke verdient, hält er geheim. Diskretion! Bemerkenswert ist ohnehin eine andere Zahl: Lukas Mielke ist erst 18 Jahre alt. „Wenn ich 30 bin, möchte ich fünf Jahre lang um die Welt segeln. Das ist mein großes Ziel", sagt er.

In der elften Klasse gründet Mielke das erste Unternehmen, vertreibt Nahrungsergänzungsmittel und Kosmetika. Das einfache Prinzip: billig einkaufen, teuer verkaufen. Heute hat er knapp 40 Mitarbeiter, sein Geschäft hat er längst ausgeweitet auf Webdesign und den Handel mit Solaranlagen. Die Schule absolviert er nebenbei, macht Fernabitur und besucht gleichzeitig erste Wirtschaftsvorlesungen an der Uni.

Mielke weiß, dass er anders ist als viele seiner Altersgenossen. Er hat erkannt, dass er arbeiten muss, wenn er etwas haben will: „Ich leiste lieber jetzt etwas und ruhe mich später aus."

Vorurteile von Gleichaltrigen? Ja, das gebe es schon, sagt Mielke: „Aber ich habe das Gefühl, dass da oft Neid dahintersteckt." Im Job wird sein Alter manchmal ein Problem, sagt Lukas: „Wenn ich einen, der die doppelte Lebenserfahrung hat, von einem Geschäft überzeugen will, ist das schon schwierig."

Quelle: ddp

Zeda: Rapperin

Rap und Hiphop sind die Musik vieler Migrantenjugendlicher und Kinder aus der sozialen Unterschicht. Die Lyrics der deutsch-libanesischen Rapperin Zeda erzählen von Wut, Schmerz und Glück. Sie hat sich in der Männerwelt des Hiphop ihren Platz erkämpft – und das alles ohne Management.

Das gerade einmal 1,55 Meter große Energiebündel ist ein aufgehender Stern am Frankfurter Hiphop-Himmel.

Vor 20 Jahren floh ihre Familie vor dem Bürgerkrieg ins norddeutsche Peine. Dort wuchs sie in einem sozialen Brennpunkt auf, wurde eingeschult, ohne ein Wort Deutsch zu sprechen. Zeda sang in der Schulband, Songs von den Rolling Stones zum Beispiel. Das wollte die Lehrerin. Aber für Zeda passte das nicht. „Singen ist zu sehr heile Welt, diese extremen Gefühle lassen sich nur in Sprachgesang ausdrücken", sagt sie. „Hiphop ist ein Lebensgefühl, es ist meine Sprache."

Peine ließ ihr keinen Raum, sich zu entfalten. So packte Zeda ihre Koffer und suchte eine Wohnung in Frankfurt am Main, lebte zunächst vom Ersparten. Sie klappert die Hiphop-Läden ab, zieht zum Freestylen durch Bars und Clubs und lernt andere Künstler kennen.

Leben kann Zeda noch nicht von ihrer Musik. Ihren Lebensunterhalt verdient sie in einer Apotheke, Vollzeit. Dennoch nimmt sie sich Zeit für Jugendliche: In Workshops bringt sie ihnen bei, Texte zu schreiben und zu „performen". Ehrenamtlich.

Quelle: Ludwig Michaela

✲ Writing Part 3: Mediation – Young Careers

Your class is taking part in a European project called "Young Careers" and you have to write a text in English about a young German's professional development.
- Read the two articles.
- Choose **one** article.
- Say what the person does and mention at least four **important** aspects of their professional development.
- **Do not translate word for word**, just give the main information.
- Write complete sentences.

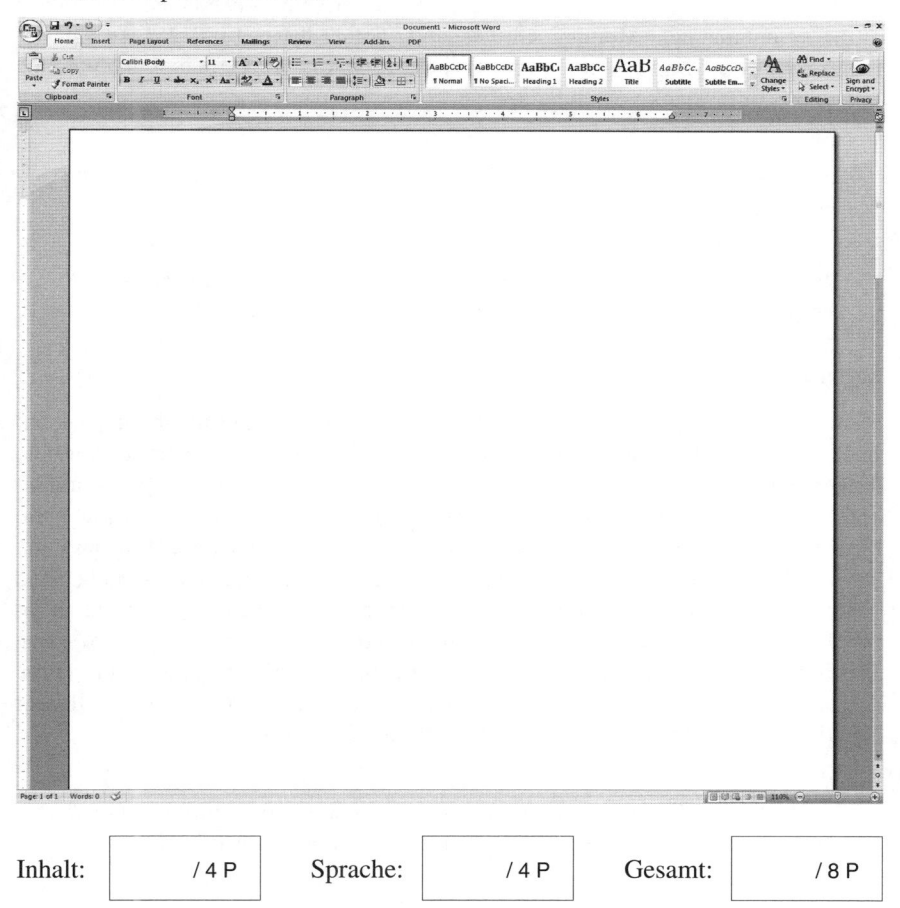

Inhalt: ___ / 4 P   Sprache: ___ / 4 P   Gesamt: ___ / 8 P

2015-23

Lösungsvorschläge

Listening Part 1: Short Messages

Message One

Hello, this is Taylor Benson from Cleveland, Ohio. I ordered some items from your online store last week; the order no. is TB/1244/01. I got the delivery yesterday but there's a problem, I'm afraid. The hiking shoes are the wrong size. You've sent me size 7, which is too small, I need one size bigger. Would you please send another pair as soon as possible? It's really urgent because I need them for my trip to the mountains next Monday. Oh yes, and another thing, I ordered ten pairs of tennis socks but you've sent me soccer socks instead. Please get in touch with me to sort this out. Thank you and goodbye.

1. B
   Hinweis: "You've sent me size 7, which is too small, I need one size bigger." (Z. 3/4)

2. C
   Hinweis: "... I need them for my trip to the mountains next Monday." (Z. 5/6)

Message Two

Hello, it's Mark Spencer from the Blueberry Lodge. I'm calling about your online reservation. I'm sorry to tell you that the two beds in the 4-bed dorm are no longer available on the dates you want. The only room we can offer you is a double room with a double bed, which costs € 25 per person per night. I know it's a bit more expensive than the dorm but then you'll have your own bathroom and shower. Breakfast is included in the price. All guests have free use of kitchen and barbecue facilities. If you need to wash your clothes, there's a coin-operated washing machine in the basement. You can buy the coins at the reception. There's free Wi-Fi throughout the lodge. You can also rent bikes for free but please let us know one day in advance, so we can arrange this for you. I hope I could answer all your questions and we look forward to your booking. Bye for now.

3. B
   Hinweis: "The only room we can offer you is a double room with a double bed ... but then you'll have your own bathroom and shower." (Z. 3–6)

4. A
   Hinweis: "... there's a coin-operated washing machine in the basement. You can buy the coins at the reception." (Z. 7/8)

Listening Part 2: Radio Ads

Ad 1: School

1 What do you think your kid is going to do without graduating from high school? It's up to me to make sure my son gets to class on time. Not just because it's my responsibility and the law, but because I want the best for my child. So, I ask about his grades and I encourage him to stay on track. Because missing even one
5 day every few weeks can prevent him from graduating. So I remind him: The more you learn, the more you earn.
School – it pays to stay. Visit dc.gov/stayinschool

DC.gov, District of Columbia, licensed under CC BY 3.0 US

5. B
Hinweis: "It's up to me to make sure my son gets to class on time ... Because missing even one day every few weeks can prevent him from graduating." (Z. 2–5)

Ad 2: Campfire

1 SON: Hey, nice campfire, dad.
FATHER: I am the woodsman. Shall we hike to the waterfall before dark?
SON: What about your campfire?
FATHER: It'll be okay until we get back.
5 SON: No, it won't. Sparks will make it start a wildfire and burn this whole area. Then we'd get the bill for any damages and for putting it out.
FATHER: Oh ...!
SON: Let's roast hot dogs now, woodsman and see the waterfall tomorrow.
A message from the Minnesota Department of Natural Resources.

© (2013) State of Minnesota, Department of Natural Resources

6. C
Hinweis: "Sparks will make it start a wildfire and burn this whole area. Then we'd get the bill for any damages and for putting it out." (Z. 5/6)

Ad 3: Oil

1 *(Gurgling sound of pouring something into a cup)*
MAN: Hey, what are you doing?
WOMAN: Oops, you caught me.
MAN: You bet I caught you. What's this gunk you put into my coffee?
5 WOMAN: Oh, just some motor oil.
MAN: Motor oil! What are you tryin' to do? Kill me?

WOMAN: No, but remember when you changed your oil last week? You poured the old oil into the empty lot. And I said that's wrong because the oil would sink into the ground and could end up in our water some day.
MAN: What?!
WOMAN: And do you remember what you said?
MAN: What?
WOMAN: You said: "As long as nobody knows, what's the difference?"
MAN: What's that got to do with putting oil into my coffee?
WOMAN: Hey, as long as nobody knows, what's the difference?
MAN: What?
WOMAN: Your words, baby.
SPEAKER: So what if nobody knows you did it? That oil could still end up in our water. Next time you change your oil and filter, call 1-888-Clean-LA and we'll give you the location of a collection center near you – at a gas station or auto parts store. Please, do your part because the reality is 50 percent of oil sold is never collected. This message is funded by a grant from the California Integrated Waste Management Board and Project Pollution Prevention.

Los Angeles County Department of Public Works

7. F
   Hinweis: "That oil could still end up in our water ... Please, do your part because the reality is 50 percent of oil sold is never collected." (Z. 18–22)

Ad 4: Photography

This is the sound of an amateur photographer: *(camera shutter click)*
And this is the sound of a professional photographer: *(click)*
Once again, that's amateur: *(click)* – and professional: *(click)*
If you are currently a *(click)* and interested in a career as a *(click)*, learn what makes the difference with a bachelor of photography from Queensland College of Art, Griffith University. To find out more, simply google Griffith photography – the QCA where *(click)* become *(click)*.

JuniorCru

8. A
   Hinweis: "If you are currently a (click) and interested in a career as a (click), learn what makes the difference with a bachelor of photography from Queensland College of Art, Griffith University." (Z. 4–6)

Listening Part 3: World Alternative Games

Hello everyone and welcome to the World Alternative Games, here in Llanwrtyd Wells, the smallest town in Wales. *(cheering crowd)* Yes, ladies and gentlemen the excitement is rising – the stiletto race will start at any moment. If you think that walking or standing in high heels – stilettos – is a pain, maybe you should try running in them. This is what the race is all about. Now, I have no idea where this craze started but it has become very popular all over Europe. For those of you who have never heard of such nonsense: this is racing while wearing high-heeled shoes. The running distance is 55 metres. Oh, and before you ask ... YES, men may also compete. There are a few simple rules though: Racers must bring their own shoes and boots are not allowed. Shoes must have heels of a minimum of 7 centimetres. You'll be disqualified if you turn up in your 1970s platform heels.
(Bang)
And off they go!
(Pause)
And now I'm here at the wife carrying competition. This is a sport that started in Finland a long time ago. Don't the contestants look great in their colourful outfits? But it's not just fun and games. Imagine how difficult it must be for them to balance their wives on their backs. Just in case ... the wives are wearing protective helmets on their heads. The aim of this game is that men carry their wives through an obstacle course that includes sand, water and fences. The obstacle course is 254 metres long. That's quite a long distance. I'm not sure if I would manage to cross the finish line. By the way, competing couples do not have to be married. However, participants must be at least 21 years old. And same-sex couples are allowed. Oops, and here the first wife is falling ...
(Geräusch: Platschen und raunende Menge)
(Pause)
And now I'm over here at one of the wackiest competitions in the whole world – the egg throwing tournament. This is a crazy game of throwing and catching raw eggs. It all started in Greece when the Greeks threw eggs at the Persians back in 480 BC. Don't ask me why ...
At any moment now the teams will enter the arena wearing safety goggles and orange raincoats with hoods. Teams are made up of 2 people and the idea is to throw a raw egg at your partner WITHOUT breaking it. The first team has already taken their position standing 10 metres apart from each other to start the contest. As long as the egg doesn't break, the team can go on to the next round, each time moving another 5 metres apart. I think the current world record is around 70 metres. Participants must be aware of the following rules: The organiser will provide the eggs. Players may not use any help when catching or throw-

ing eggs. This includes any kind of glove, net or instrument that would give an unfair advantage to the team. What an egg-centric game. But I think I'll get out of here before things get messy. *(Sound of eggs breaking)*

Based on: http://www.worldalternativegames.co.uk/11.09.2013

9. high heels/stilettos (Z. 4)/high-heeled shoes (Z. 7/8)

10. 55 (Z. 8)

11. men may compete (Z. 9)/(bring your) own shoes (Z. 9/10)/ boots not allowed (Z. 10)/heels of (minimum) 7 cm (Z. 10/11)

12. Finland (Z. 16/17)

13. colourful outfits (Z. 17/18)/(protective) helmets (for wives) (Z. 19/20)

14. 254 (Z. 22)

15. Greece (Z. 30)

16. (safety) goggles/glasses (Z. 32)/(orange) raincoats (with hoods) (Z. 33)

17. teams of 2 people (Z. 33)/throw egg without breaking it (Z. 34)/stand ten metres apart (Z. 35)/organiser provides eggs (Z. 38/39)/no glove/no net/ no instrument (Z. 40/41)

Listening Part 4: Fast Fashion

TALMA: This is Talma Williams from British Radio, and welcome to our weekly edition of "Have Your Say!" Today we're talking about "fast fashion", also known as McFashion. That's when designer trends are brought into the shops as fast and as cheap as possible.

But before we get into our discussion, let me introduce my guests: here is Malvin Kureishi, a young man from London, who is 16 years old and just loves shopping.

MALVIN: Yo, that's me.

TALMA: Also here with us is Hannah Flynn ..., a former fast-fashion junkie, who has written "Stop Before You Shop", a behind-the-scenes book on "fast fashion".

HANNAH: Hi. Thanks for having me.

TALMA: And last but not least we have Bill Wallace, founder of the British clothing chain Zady and number three this year on the Forbes billionaire list.

BILL: Hello. I'm pleased to be here.

TALMA: So Malvin, you love shopping, don't you? How often do you go to the shops?

MALVIN: At least once a week ... That way I can get something new to wear every Saturday night.
TALMA: Really?
MALVIN: Yeah, I want to make a statement with the clothes I wear. And I know exactly where to find the right gear at the right price. Some people think shopping is a waste of time but I love it! I actually get a real kick out of it. I mean BINGO – that moment when I spot the perfect T-shirt for a perfect price. Then I rush home and – I make a haul video. And that's when, for the first time, I actually wear the T-shirt. Yo! JUST LOVE IT!
TALMA: *(laughing)* Now, if you are not a shopper! But Malvin, what's a "haul video"?
MALVIN: You don't know what a haul video is? Well, it's when you turn on your webcam and film yourself unpacking your shopping bags and presenting all the cool things you've bought. And when you're finished, you post the video on the Internet.
TALMA: Why bother doing something like that?
MALVIN: Never really thought about it – all my friends do it ... It's just fun ... *(smiling)* maybe a bit of showing off ... I think I've even heard that some people make money out of it. I mean, some shops pay to have their products presented in haul videos.
TALMA: Sounds like a clever form of advertising. Bill, that must be music to your ears.
BILL: It certainly is. And it's also one of the reasons why my clothing company, Zady, doesn't need to spend much on advertising. We don't even have a proper marketing department any more.
TALMA: Bill, you are probably the most successful man I've ever had on this show. You've literally gone from rags to riches. What is the secret of your success?
BILL: Well, it's actually all because of the fast fashion trend Malvin has just described. We are the ones who bring the trendy fashion into the shops faster and cheaper than most other companies. We're able to get the Prada look into the shops even before Prada does. And we also make sure that there is a fast turnover of articles in our shops so that customers like Malvin keep coming back to buy more. While other clothing chains have new designs in the shops four times a year, we have new ones every two weeks. That means that every year we introduce about 10,000 new designs.
HANNAH: *(condescending/ironic)* Trendier, cheaper and faster. But what you're actually doing is simply copying designs from fashion houses and selling these ... these knockoff clothes for next to nothing. Come on, there is no such thing as cheap clothes. As I point out in my book, somebody does pay in the long run. And in the clothing industry it's not the consumers who pay the

real price. It's the women or children who work in these terrible sweatshops in countries like Bangladesh. They have to work long hours in awful working conditions to produce these outfits in no time at all.

BILL: Wait a minute, let me get this point straight: most of what we sell in Europe is also produced here in Europe. And if we really have to outsource to some place in Asia, we make sure the working conditions are up to standard.

HANNAH: Well, it's good to hear you're taking that aspect seriously, but there's much more to this whole story. Just think of the environmental consequences. Shoppers often wear these new clothes only once or twice before throwing them away.

TALMA: What a waste! That's not very sustainable, is it?

BILL: Maybe not, but you know how fast trends change. And Talma, I'm a businessman and what I do is provide the masses with exclusive designs at a good price. It's what I call the democratisation of luxury. I dress the man or woman on the street in the latest fashion. But, at the end of the day it's the customers' decision to buy a garment or not.

TALMA: So Hannah, if it's up to the customers, how can we be more ethical when shopping for clothes?

HANNAH: Well, first of all we should think about buying less. All of us buy more than we need. And you know when I actually started to change my shopping habits? It was the day I found clothes in my wardrobe with the price tags still on them.

MALVIN: Oh ... that would never happen to me.

HANNAH: Let me tell you what I personally do: I check a company's reputation to make sure that it isn't connected to sweatshops in places like Asia and that it has a transparency policy. And lately, I've discovered some really great second-hand shops. So, why not buy second-hand clothes for a change?

TALMA: Here we definitely have some food for thought. Now it's time for a short break.

(fade out) We'll be back with more ideas on this topic after the break ...

Based on: http://learnenglish.britishcouncil.org/en/uk-culture/ethical-shopping;
http://www.ecouterre.com/zaras-way-how-fast-fashion-snared-us-with-low-prices-quick-changes/2/;
http://www.garancedore.fr/en/2013/05/29/my-new-ten-commandments-of-style-ok-five/;
http://www.youtube.com/watch?v=tHITPWn3WFg [04. 09. 2013]

18. B

Hinweis: "... Hannah Flynn ... who has written 'Stop Before You Shop', a behind-the-scenes book on 'fast fashion'." (Z. 9–11)

19. A
   Hinweis:
   TALMA: "... How often do you go to the shops?"
   MALVIN: "At least once a week ..." (Z. 16–18)

20. A
   Hinweis: "Then I rush home and – I make a haul video." (Z. 25); "... you turn on your webcam and film yourself ... presenting all the cool things you've bought." (Z. 29–31)

21. C
   Hinweis: "We are the ones who bring the trendy fashion into the shops faster and cheaper than most other companies." (Z. 47/48)

22. A
   Hinweis: "It's the women or children who work in these terrible sweatshops in countries like Bangladesh. They have to work long hours in awful working conditions to produce these outfits in no time at all." (Z. 59–61)

23. B
   Hinweis: "... what I do is provide the masses with exclusive designs at a good price. It's what I call the democratisation of luxury." (Z. 71/72)

24. C
   Hinweis: "... check a company's reputation to make sure that it isn't connected to sweatshops in places like Asia and that it has a transparency policy." (Z. 82–84); "Well, first of all we should think about buying less. All of us buy more than we need." (Z. 77/78)

25. A
   Hinweis: "Come on, there is no such thing as cheap clothes ... somebody does pay in the long run. And in the clothing industry it's not the consumers who pay the real price. It's the women or children who work in these terrible sweatshops in countries like Bangladesh." (Z. 56–60); "Just think of the environmental consequences. Shoppers often wear these new clothes only once or twice before throwing them away." (Z. 66–68)

Reading Part 1: Watching TV

1./2. **B, C**
Hinweis: Raju is "... a construction worker from Pakistan ...", "... likes watching funny series about immigrant families.", "... likes to watch programmes that have something to do with his job."
→ programme B: "... sitcom about the British-Pakistani Khans ..."
→ programme C: "... mobile crane company ..."

3./4. **E, F**
Hinweis: Sami "... is working on a presentation about the situation of homosexuals in different countries ...", "... works as a dogsitter and is naturally interested in finding out as much as possible about these furry friends."
→ programme E: "... Brazil, home to the largest gay pride celebration", "... one gay person is murdered every 36 hours in Brazil."
→ programme F: "The Wonder of Dogs", "... looks at the special relationship between people and dogs."

5./6. **C, F**
Hinweis: Grace and her husband "... like to watch programmes with some heavy construction going on.", Grace "... enjoys touching stories about pets and their owners."
→ programme C: "... mobile crane company ...", "... huge machines ... carrying out the biggest lifts of all."
→ programme F: "... looks at the special relationship between people and dogs."

7./8. **B, D**
Hinweis: Imogen "... enjoys watching comedies with lots of good jokes.", "... loves animals and is especially interested in helping endangered ones."
→ programme B: "You will laugh yourself sick."
→ programme D: "Many animals are in danger because of alien invaders, or as a result of our tidying up and building on the countryside.", "... shows how you can help ..."

9./10. **A, G**
Hinweis: Shaniqua "... shows great interest in landscape photography.", "... is also interested in programmes that she can relate to, for example the situation at home – her older brother doesn't want to move out of his comfort zone."

→ *programme A:* "This documentary about spring in Britain is packed with beautiful photography."
→ *programme G:* "Hotel of Mum and Dad"

Reading Part 2: Short Texts

11. D

   Hinweis: "... do not hold the door open for anyone who does not have a tower ticket."

12. A

   Hinweis: "Caution: Loose and Missing Stepping Stones."

13. C

   Hinweis: "PLEASE RESPECT THE BOATS"

14. B

   Hinweis: "He started going to school every day, getting to class on time and turning in his assignments. His hard work paid off; he is getting A's and is headed for college."

15. A

   Hinweis: "For your added security video cameras are being introduced on London Underground trains"

16. A

   Hinweis: "... teaming the most highly trained dogs with firefighters to save lives. To donate, call (888) 459-4376 ..."

Reading Part 3: Educating Yorkshire

17. D

   Hinweis: "Georgia is a 16-year-old with a lousy attitude; she swears at the teachers, won't wear her school uniform and storms out of class when she's told off." (Z. 1/2), "... her teachers ... are proud that she is going to take her GCSEs." (Z. 4/5)

18. D

   Hinweis: "... from teachers' meetings in the staff room to pupils dancing at the school prom." (Z. 9/10), "... young Asian girl working really hard for her GCSEs ..." (Z. 11)

19. C

    Hinweis: "Thornhill, a former failing school, is now rated 'good' in school inspections. It was expected to get 45 per cent A–C grades at GCSE last year but it actually managed 63 per cent." (Z. 23–25)

20. D

    Hinweis: "In the first 20 minutes the kids did not show any respect." (Z. 30/31)

21. C

    Hinweis: "… generally, behaviour improved a bit." (Z. 34/35)

22. B

    Hinweis: " 'A lot of our families are financially deprived but they all want to keep up with each other. They spend shedloads on a dress … It's bonkers.' " (Z. 45–47)

23. B

    Hinweis: "Over 100 schools volunteered to be featured, and it took ten months for Thornhill to be chosen …" (Z. 48/49)

24. C

    Hinweis: "… sometimes the teachers as well as the pupils are seen making mistakes. 'It shows humanity,' says Jonny." (Z. 55/56)

25. D

    Hinweis: Der Artikel befasst sich nur sehr indirekt mit dem Thema „Medienerziehung heute" – Überschrift B scheidet daher aus. Es geht auch nicht nur um den Schuldirektor (Überschrift A) oder die Lehrerschaft (Überschrift C). Stattdessen steht das Schulleben insgesamt im Vordergrund – Überschrift D passt daher am besten.

Writing Part 1: A New Soap Character

Name of character: z. B. Daniel Johnson
Age: z. B. 28 years
z. B.: Male

1. z. B. architect
2. z. B. sailing, playing the guitar
3. positive quality: z. B. helpful; negative quality: z. B. impatient
4. z. B. has saved a person's life
5. z. B. organize a charity

Writing Part 2: Mobile Phones

Hinweis: Lies dir die E-Mail des Bloggers genau durch – es werden insgesamt vier Aspekte genannt, auf die du in deiner Lösung eingehen musst. Zunächst musst du ausführen, ob bzw. unter welchen Umständen man an deiner Schule Handys verwenden darf. Danach schilderst du kurz, was passiert, wenn man diese Regeln bricht. Als letztes musst du auf Vor- und Nachteile der Handynutzung in der Schule eingehen.

Hi Fony,

At my school mobile phones aren't permitted either. We are also going to have a new headmaster next year, and I hope he will do something about changing the rules. As it is now, if you use your mobile within the school building, the teacher will take your phone, and your parents will have to come and collect it. I think this rule is ridiculous. At other schools the punishment is that you have to bring a cake to the next class if your phone rings during the lesson. I think if you look up new words with your smartphone it's a lot faster and more fun than using those old-fashioned dictionaries. On the other hand, the only negative thing is that mobile phones can really become addictive and that many students don't pay attention in class or don't really talk to each other anymore during the breaks.

Hope this helps,

(your name)   (152 words)

Writing Part 3: Mediation – Young Careers

Hinweis: Hier hast du zwei Themen zur Auswahl – wähle am besten denjenigen Artikel aus, über den du am leichtesten auf Englisch schreiben kannst. Insgesamt musst du in deiner Lösung auf mindestens vier Stationen im beruflichen Werdegang des Jungunternehmers bzw. der Rapperin eingehen.

Beispiellösung zu Lukas Mielke:

Lukas Mielke is a young businessman. His company has got 40 employees and he's always very busy. He founded his first company when he was in grade 11. He began by selling food supplements and cosmetics, but later expanded, specializing in web design and solar panels. His business principle is "buy low and sell high". He's still working on his A-levels and attending university courses in economics at the same time. His dream is to work hard now and retire early. But this is difficult because he has to compete with more experienced business people.

(95 words)

Beispiellösung zu Zeda:

Zeda is a female rapper with Lebanese roots who wants to make it in the male-dominated rapper world. She's a rising star in Frankfurt's hip-hop scene, and she doesn't have a manager. When she started school in Peine, she didn't speak a word of German and began singing in a school band. Later she moved to Frankfurt where she performed in bars and clubs and met other hip-hoppers. She isn't a professional yet and has to work full-time in a pharmacy to get by. In spite of that, Zeda uses her freetime to work voluntarily with young people and give hip-hop workshops. (102 words)

Bildnachweis:
S. 2015-1: Joggerin © Can Stock Photo Inc./bogdanhoda; Tennisspielerin © Can Stock Photo Inc./JanPietruszka; S. 2015-2: Wanderin © My Good Images. Shutterstock; Fußballspielerinnen © Fotokostic. Shutterstock; Waschmaschine © Dan Jonut Popescu; Fahrrad © Dudarev Mikhail. Shutterstock; Grill © K. Miri Photography. Shutterstock; WiFi © Can Stock Photo Inc./Oakozhan; S. 2015-3: Stereoanlage © PRILL Mediendesign/fotolia.de; S. 2015-4: Stiletto Racing © shootingankauf – Fotolia.com; Wife Carrying © Steve Jurvetson, lizenziert unter CC BY 2.0 (Bild wurde zugeschnitten); Egg Throwing: gemeinfrei; S. 2015-5: junger Mann mit Einkaufstüten © Wrangel/Dreamstime.com; S. 2015-8: "Raju" © Can Stock Photo Inc./szefei; "Sami" © Can Stock Photo Inc./soupstock; "Grace" © 123rf.com; S. 2015-9: "Imogen" © Can Stock Photo Inc./martinbalo; "Shaniqua" © Can Stock Photo Inc./galinast; S. 2015-10: Vogel © 123rf.com; Citizen Khan, reproduced under licence from BBC One © 2012 BBC; Arbeiter vor Kran © Can Stock Photo Inc./wayne0216; Wald © Subbotina Anna. Shutterstock; S. 2015-11: Stephen Fry © Copyright Sprout Pictures; Mann und Hund © Can Stock Photo Inc./miss_j; Hotel of Mum and Dad © Mentornmedia; S. 2015-13: Schuhe © Can Stock Photo Inc./Jurij; S. 2015-14: Hundepfote © Photographer Deborah Samuels who donated her creative photo. Young & Rubicam, New York – Marketing and Communication Firm; S. 2015-15: Educating Yorkshire © http://tangerine-digital-pr.blogspot.de/2013/09/educating-yorkshire-valuable-lesson-in.html; S. 2015-20: Daumen hoch/Daumen runter © Can Stock Photo Inc./ RedKoala; S. 2015-21: Cartoon-Junge mit Handy © Can Stock Photo Inc./cthoman; S. 2015-22: Lukas Mielke © picture alliance/AP Images; Zeda © Zeda

> Schriftliche Prüfung zum MSA und zur eBBR in Berlin/Brandenburg
> Englisch 2016

Listening Part 1: Short Messages

- You are going to hear two short messages.
- You will hear the recording twice.
- There are four questions in this part, two questions for each message.
- Look at the pictures and then listen to the recording.
- Choose the correct picture and put a tick (✓) in the right box.

Message One

1. What kind of job is Jakob interested in?

   A ☐   B ☐

   C ☒   D ☐

2. At what time can Jakob come for the interview?

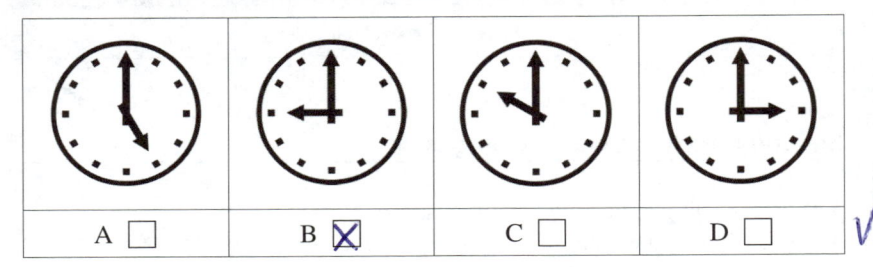

A ☐   B ☒   C ☐   D ☐   ✓

Message Two

3. What are you NOT allowed to bring inside the museum?

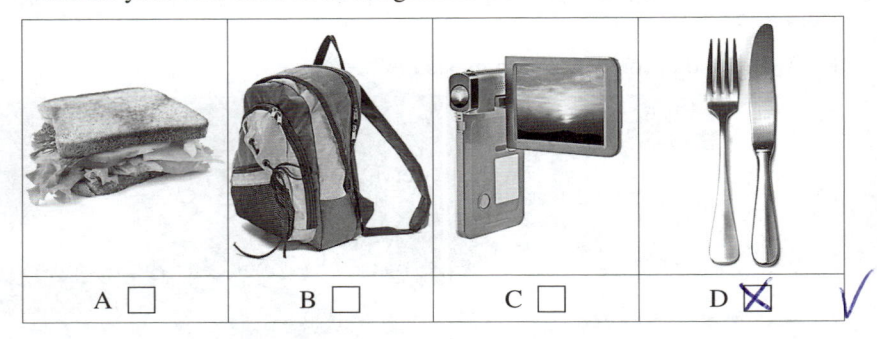

A ☐   B ☐   C ☐   D ☒   ✓

4. Which part of the museum is NOT open to the public?

A ☐   B ☒   ✓

C ☐   D ☐

Listening Part 2: Radio Ads

Please note: You do not need to understand every word to do this task.

- You are going to hear four radio ads.
- You will hear the recording twice.
- Read the slogans below first, then listen to the recording.
- For each ad choose the correct slogan from the list (A–F) and put a tick (✓) in the right box.
- There is only one correct slogan for each ad.
- Two slogans can't be matched.

A   Read a book – find your way to someone's heart ✓
B   Switch off the light – save energy
C   Follow these rules – keep your home safe
D   A healthy life – it only takes a few steps ✓
E   Exercise right – see your doctor first
F   Turn it off – spend time with your loved ones ✓

				Slogan			
	Radio Ads	A	B	C	D	E	F
5.	Radio Ad 1				X			✓
6.	Radio Ad 2						X	✓
*7.| Radio Ad 3	X						✓
8.	Radio Ad 4			X				✓

2016-3

Listening Part 3: Schools Around the World

- You are going to hear three reports about different schools.
- You will hear the recording twice.
- Complete the table below. Use 1 to 5 words or numbers for each answer.

	Country	Age of students	👍 Likes (Name one)	👉 Dislikes (Name one)
Class Afloat		9. 16-17 years	*10. seeing other cultures and landscapes / seeing sights	11. - cleaning the deck - extreme weather conditions
Summerhill School	12. east of England	5-18	13. - fun school - equality for everyone	*14. teachers don't plan lessons carefully
Padamu Education Centre	15. Bangladesh	6-10	16. - free meal & school material	17. homesickness

2016-4

Listening Part 4: Hotel Mom and Dad

- You are going to hear a radio show.
- There are four people in the show: Sally Jessy Raphael (the host), Sam Maynard, Maria Maynard and Andrew Chan.
- You will hear the recording twice.
- Read the statements below first, then listen to the recording.
- Put a tick (✓) in the box next to the correct statement.
- Only one statement is correct in each case.

18. Maria Maynard wanted her children …
    A ☐ to stay at home until they got married.
    B ☒ to move out as soon as they became adults. ✓
    C ☐ to finish school before moving out.

19. Sam moved back home because …
    A ☐ he was waiting for a place at college.
    B ☐ his girlfriend liked the comfort of his family home. ✓
    C ☒ he did not want to spend so much on living costs.

20. According to Andrew Chan, a consequence of young adults living with their parents is that …
    A ☐ they get lazy and depressed.
    B ☒ they do not develop important financial skills. ✓
    C ☐ they become socially isolated.

* 21. Sam's parents …
    A ☒ pay some of his regular bills. ✓
    B ☐ have bought him a new car.
    C ☐ pay his college fees.

* 22. What is Andrew Chan's advice to parents?
    A ☐ Save money for your children's future.
    B ☒ Set up rules about money matters. ✓
    C ☐ Always keep an eye on your children's spendings.

* 23. Why might grown children be a problem for their parents?
    - A ☐ Parents might develop serious health problems.
    - B ☐ Parents' relationships might suffer.
    - C ☒ Parents might face financial problems in the future.

* 24. How does Maria feel about her son still living at home?
    - A ☐ She wants him to move out as soon as possible because she needs his room.
    - B ☒ She feels that her freedom in her own house is limited.
    - C ☐ She does not mind having him around the house as long as he takes his studies seriously.

* 25. Which statement sums up this part of the talk show best?
    - A ☐ Boomerang kids are a product of overprotective parents.
    - B ☒ Boomerang kids have problems growing up.
    - C ☐ Boomerang kids have a close relationship with their parents.

Listening: Candidate Answer Sheet   Name: _____

For students: Put a tick (✓) in the correct box.

Part 1: Short Messages

Number	A	B	C	D
1				
2				
3				
4				

/ 4 P

Part 2: Radio Ads

Number	Radio Ads	Slogan					
		A	B	C	D	E	F
5	Radio Ad 1						
6	Radio Ad 2						
*7	Radio Ad 3						
8	Radio Ad 4						

/ 4 P

Part 3: Schools Around the World

Die Ergebnisse müssen nicht übertragen werden (*10 und *14).

/ 9 P

Part 4: Hotel Mom and Dad

Number	A	B	C
18			
19			
20			
*21			
*22			
*23			
*24			
*25			

/ 8 P

/ 25 P

2016-7

Reading Part 1: Apps

- These people (a–e) want to download some useful apps onto their phones.
- First read the information about the people, then look at the descriptions of the apps (A–G) on pages 10 and 11.
- In each case (a–e) find the **two** apps the people would download. Write the letters of the apps in the boxes next to the people's names.
- Some of the apps can be chosen more than once.

No.	App 1	App 2		The people
1/2				a) **Jamal** has seen better days. Over the past three months he has gained a few kilos and he has performed pretty badly at school. But now he wants to change that. What he needs is a cool running app that keeps him away from the couch and one that helps him remember to do his homework.
3/4				b) **Afifa** trains the youth team of her soccer club. They are good but they don't score. So, she is looking for an app that would help her to analyze goal kicks. On the weekends she loves to go to concerts with her friends. If an app could only tell her beforehand where they all plan to go.
5/6				c) **Grace** is a festival addict who always wants to be the first to get the tickets. If there is an app she needs, it is one that makes buying and selling tickets as easy as pie. But she would also feel more comfortable at these festivals with an app that can notify her closest friends or family if necessary.

7/8

d) **Ryan**
has to take a 30-minute train ride to school. Instead of staring out of the window he would like to listen to news stories or blogs but this app has not been designed yet, or has it? Especially in the evening he has already experienced some dangerous situations on the train. Some friends could easily help him out if he could contact them somehow.

9/10

e) **Charlotte**
has just moved into town from Berlin, Germany. She needs to work on her English a little. An app that explains music clips or talk shows would be great for her. Listening to some authentic speakers who read the news in an app would be a perfect exercise, too. Here she could see how much she already understands.

A) Are you one of the people who never really have the time to sit down and read the newspaper or a blog? This might be <u>the</u> app for you. Listen to an ever growing catalogue of articles from the world's best publishers and bloggers narrated by professional voice-actors. Whether commuting, working out at the gym, or cooking at home, let this app accompany you and enrich your day. This app is perfect for you if you like podcasts, listen to audio books or prefer to consume other audio content on the go.

B) This is a video app for serious athletes who want to improve their performance in sports. Record and analyze amazing HD videos and instantly review them in slow motion. Create and share coaching videos that help you train smarter and see results faster. Record your players and instantly show them how to improve, right on the field. Analyze your golf swing, easily break down a volleyball serve, improve soccer skills, or even demonstrate proper weightlifting. Every coach, parent and athlete needs this app.

C) With this app you will run like never before. If you find it hard to work up the motivation to exercise, try being chased by a rampaging zombie horde. Using either pedometer step tracking or (less accurate) GPS, this app makes a game out of exercising with a storyline played over your headphones. Each "episode" can be infused with songs from your personal playlist. As you run, you'll find items and earn points which can be used to upgrade your base and, just maybe, help humanity survive the zombie apocalypse.

D) Discover popular local events, get event recommendations just for you, and see which events your friends are going to! Get tickets and quickly access all of your tickets and event information from your phone. Find something new to do – concerts, festivals, classes, conferences, free events and more – right in the palm of your hand. This app enables anyone to create, promote, and sell tickets to any event imaginable, while also helping people discover and share events that match their passions – whether it's a neighborhood block party or a sold-out concert.

E) This app does not do your school work for you. Instead, it allows you to stay organized and on top of your assignments through a handy calendar function that allows you to enter class times, homework assignments and study sessions. The app also lets you set reminders so you never forget what assignments and reading you need to complete. For example, if you have a class on Tuesday and need to read two chapters of your textbook by Monday night, the app will send you a reminder on the day of your choosing so you can stay ahead of the game.

F) This unique app is for those situations when you need to quickly and discreetly get help from your friends or family. Two quick taps sends one of three pre-written text messages to as many as six of your contacts. One message sends your GPS location and a request to be picked up, while another asks your friends to quickly get in touch with you. With this app you have a new way to connect with your most trusted friends – to stay close, stay safe and prevent violence before it happens!

G) This app takes real-world videos and turns them into English learning experiences. You'll learn English as it's spoken in real life.
Browse through the huge database of the app and find the latest music videos, popular talk shows, news, inspiring talks and funny commercials. This app makes it really easy to watch English videos. There are captions that are interactive. That means you can tap on any word to see an image, definition, and useful examples. Learning by watching has never been so easy.

Reading Part 2: Short Texts

- Look at the text and the statements in each task.
- What does the text say?
- Put a tick (✓) next to the statement that matches the text – **A**, **B**, **C** or **D**.
- There is only one correct statement for each sign.

*11.

Monday, March 9, 2016 **METRO**

To the gorgeous conductor on the Arriva Trains Wales Aberystwyth service, Polly, you brighten my day with your smile. Next time you check my ticket we should swap numbers.

What does the writer want?

A ☐ to go to Wales
B ☐ to improve the train service
C ☐ to return a lost ticket
D ☒ to get to know somebody

12.

"The smartest card in my wallet? It's a library card."
LUOL DENG

Two-time NBA all star of the Chicago Bulls, Deng, has won the NBA's Sportsmanship Award.

PUBLIC LIBRARY CARD

A ☐ Win a basketball season ticket.
B ☐ The latest book about the Chicago Bulls is available now.
C ☒ Get a library card just like Luol Deng.
D ☐ The Chicago Bulls will be giving autographs in the library.

13.

A DANGEROUS Mix

It's a fact that many fire deaths are caused by people attempting to cook or smoke while under the influence of alcohol. There's more to responsible drinking than taking a cab. Don't put yourself – or your family – at risk to fire.

This sign tells people how to prevent …

A ☐ getting drunk.
B ☒ a fire.
C ☐ a car accident.
D ☐ drug addiction.

14.

IMPORTANT ADVICE FROM THE OFFICE OF THE SURGEON GENERAL
Here's a tool to improve your health.

Exercise is Medicine®

The nation's top public health physician wants you to know: Exercise greatly reduces serious risks to your health. Simply increasing your physical activity a little can help you and your family prevent many illnesses and improve your health, fitness and well-being.

A ☒ Get moving!
B ☐ Take your daily vitamins!
C ☐ Register for the local marathon!
D ☐ See your doctor regularly!

15. **The dinosaurs are on holiday**

The *Dinosaurs* gallery is closed from 8 to 19 September for a big summer clean.

Need a dinosaur today? You can see dinosaur casts and specimens in *From the Beginning* (Red Zone), *Treasures*, *Hintze Hall* and *Fossil Marine Reptiles* (Green Zone).

You cannot visit the Dinosaurs gallery because …

A ☒ it is being cleaned.
B ☐ it is closed during the summer holidays.
C ☐ it is under construction.
D ☐ it has been moved to another museum.

16. **RUBBISH AND RECYCLING COLLECTION TIMES**

In this street we will collect your rubbish and recycling on the ✓ days below.

Monday	Tuesday	Wednesday	Thursday	Friday	Saturday	Sunday
✗	✓	✗	✗	✓	✗	✗

If you have a waste storage area please use it and do not put any waste on the pavement.

If you do not have a waste storage area please place your rubbish and recyclables, securely tied, on the pavement outside your property **before 7am** on the morning of collection. Please do not put rubbish out on any of the ✗ days.

Wrong place or wrong time and you could face enforcement action.
www.rbkc.gov.uk/wastecollections   Streetline: 020 7361 3001

THE ROYAL BOROUGH OF KENSINGTON AND CHELSEA

A ☐ You may put out your waste the night before collection.
B ☐ Use the rubbish bags that the city council provides for you.
C ☒ Both rubbish and recyclables will be collected on the same day.
D ☐ Rubbish will be collected on 5 days a week.

Reading Part 3: Distracted Walking

- Read the text and the statements on pages 17 and 18.
- Put a tick (✓) in the box next to the correct answer.
- Only one answer is correct in each case.

WASHINGTON (AP) – A young man talking on a cellphone wanders along the edge of a lonely train platform at night. Suddenly he stumbles, loses his balance and falls over the side, landing head first on the tracks. Fortunately there were no trains approaching the Philadelphia-area station at that moment, because it took the man several minutes to recover enough to climb out of danger. But the incident shows the risks of what government officials and safety experts say is a growing problem: distracted walking.

On city streets, in suburban parking lots and in shopping centers, there is usually someone walking while talking on a phone, texting with his head down, listening to music, or playing a video game. The problem isn't as widely discussed as distracted driving, but the danger is real. State and local officials are struggling to figure out how to respond, and in some cases asking how far government should go in trying to protect people from themselves.

In Delaware, highway safety officials opted for a public education campaign, placing signs on crosswalks and sidewalks at busy intersections urging pedestrians to "Look up. Drivers aren't always looking out for you."

As an April Fool's Day joke with a serious message, Philadelphia officials taped off an "e-lane" for distracted pedestrians on a sidewalk outside downtown office buildings. Some didn't get that it was a joke. "The sad part is we had people who, once they realized we were going to take the e-lane away, got mad because they thought it was really helpful to not have people get in their way while they were walking and texting," an official said.

The Utah Transit Authority adopted a regulation forbidding pedestrians from using cellphones, headphones or other distracting electronic devices while crossing the tracks of its rail system on the streets of Salt Lake City. Offenders have to pay a $50 fine. "It sounds very ridiculous," said Tia Little, a pedestrian in downtown Washington. "I mean, it's our phone. We should be able to use it and walk and talk if we choose to, walk and text or whatever."

The Southeastern Pennsylvania Transportation Authority has received reports from bus drivers and train engineers who say they nearly hit pedestrians who didn't appear to hear them sound their horns because they were distracted by their electronic devices, said Jim Fox, the agency's director of system safety and risk management.

The Internet is full of such stories: a woman texting while she walked through a suburban Philadelphia shopping mall this year tumbled into a large fountain directly in front of her and got soaking wet. A security camera video of the incident went viral, generating millions of hits.

Researchers say they're not surprised that multi-tasking pedestrians run into trouble. Psychological studies show that most people can't focus on two things at once. Instead, their attention shifts rapidly back and forth between tasks, and neither task is done well. But like a lot of drivers who use cellphones behind the wheel, pedestrians often think they're in control and that it's all the other fools on their phones who aren't watching what they're doing. "I see students as soon as they break from a class, they have their cellphones out and they're texting to one another. They're walking through the door and bumping into one another," said Jack Nasar, an Ohio State University professor and expert on environmental psychology. "People think they can do it, that they are somehow better." A study Nasar carried out on campus found that people talking on cellphones were significantly more likely to walk in front of cars than pedestrians not using phones.

In 2010, 1,500 pedestrians were treated in emergency rooms for cellphone-related incidents.

A study by researchers at Stony Brook University in New York compared the performance of people who were asked to walk across a room to a target – a piece of paper taped to the floor – without distractions and then again next day while talking on a cellphone or texting. The group that talked on the cellphone walked slightly slower and went off course a bit more than before, but the texting group walked slower, went off course 61 percent more and overshot the target 13 percent more. "People really need to be aware that they are impacting their safety by texting or talking on the cellphone" while walking, Eric Lamberg, a physical therapy professor, said. "I think the risk is there."

Joan Lowy/The Associated Press: Pedestrians distracted by electronic devices stumble into danger, raising safety concerns. In: Huffington Post, 07/30/2012. Used with permission of The Associated Press Copyright © 2016. All rights reserved.

17. What happened to the man at the railway station?
    A ☐ He took the wrong train.
    B ☐ He did not have a valid ticket.
    C ☐ He had an accident on the platform.
    D ☐ He lost his wallet.

* 18. "Distracted walking" is walking …
    A ☐ on railway tracks.
    B ☐ while using electronic devices.
    C ☐ while talking to another pedestrian.
    D ☐ both A + C

* 19. To make people watch out for the traffic, the city council of Delaware …
    A ☐ put up warnings on the side of the road.
    B ☐ forbade the use of cellphones on busy streets.
    C ☐ started an online safety campaign.
    D ☐ installed more traffic lights.

* 20. The "e-lane" in Philadelphia …
    A ☐ was not meant to be permanent.
    B ☐ was welcomed by some people.
    C ☐ caused more accidents.
    D ☐ both A + B

* 21. In Salt Lake City people are not allowed to use electronic devices …
    A ☐ in pedestrian areas.
    B ☐ in public buildings.
    C ☐ when walking across tram rails.
    D ☐ when driving.

* 22. Which incident is mentioned in ll. 29–37?
    A ☐ Someone bumped into a lamppost.
    B ☐ Someone fell down the stairs.
    C ☐ Someone fell into water.
    D ☐ Someone tripped over a suitcase.

* 23. What is said about "multitasking"?
    A ☐ Women are better at it than men.
    B ☐ People believe they themselves can do it better than others.
    C ☐ It trains people's ability to concentrate.
    D ☐ It is a new course at Ohio State University.

* 24. What did the experiment at Stony Brook University show?
    A ☐ While walking, texting is more dangerous than talking on the phone.
    B ☐ Texting while walking causes more accidents than texting while driving.
    C ☐ The more you practice texting while walking, the better you get.
    D ☐ all of them (A + B + C)

* 25. What could be the best alternative title for this article?
    A ☐ Devices down – heads up!
    B ☐ Ban distracted walking!
    C ☐ You drive, you text, you pay!
    D ☐ Freedom for phone users!

Reading: Candidate Answer Sheet   Name: _____

For students: Put a tick (✓) in the correct box.

Part 1: Apps

Number	Name	A	B	C	D	E	F	G
1/2	a) Jamal							
3/4	b) Afifa							
5/6	c) Grace							
7/8	d) Ryan							
9/10	e) Charlotte							

/ 10 P

Part 2: Short Texts

Number	A	B	C	D
*11				
12				
13				
14				
15				
16				

/ 6 P

Part 3: Distracted Walking

Number	A	B	C	D
17				
*18				
*19				
*20				
*21				
*22				
*23				
*24				
*25				

/ 9 P

/ 25 P

2016-19

Writing Part 1: Rent a Bed

- Complete the questionnaire below.
- Write keywords or short sentences.
- You may use your imagination.

Rent a Bed

We are looking for people who offer young visitors from all over the world a place to sleep in their home. Please fill out this questionnaire.

Age: 15   City/Town: Berlin / Germany

(1) Where would the visitor sleep?

In my room.

(2) Who lives with you?

My parents and my two brothers.

(3) Name two important rules in your home.

Keep everything clean, do not distract anyone from his/her work.

(4) What is nice about the area you live in?

Very central, a lot of ~~par~~ green areas.

(5) What should the visitor bring?

~~~~ His/Her own laundry

SEND   HOME

/ 5 P

Writing Part 2: Trip to Berlin

- Read what the blogger has written.
- Then write back, answering all of his questions.
- Write a minimum of 100 words.

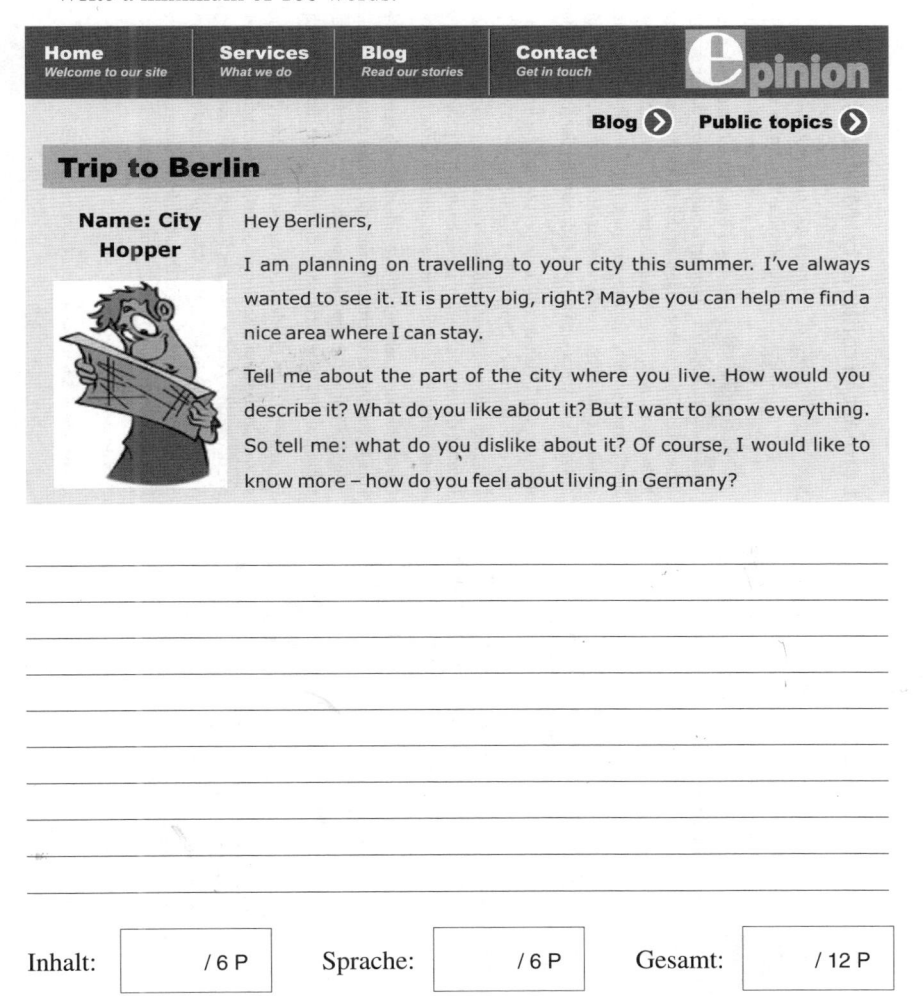

Trip to Berlin

Name: City Hopper

Hey Berliners,

I am planning on travelling to your city this summer. I've always wanted to see it. It is pretty big, right? Maybe you can help me find a nice area where I can stay.

Tell me about the part of the city where you live. How would you describe it? What do you like about it? But I want to know everything. So tell me: what do you dislike about it? Of course, I would like to know more – how do you feel about living in Germany?

Inhalt: /6 P   Sprache: /6 P   Gesamt: /12 P

★ Writing Part 3: Mediation – Young Careers

Grace Risch: Sängerin aus Berlin

Die Berliner Sängerin Grace Risch mit nigerianischen Wurzeln hat kürzlich ihre erste Single „Kleine Welt" veröffentlicht. Darin singt die 32-Jährige zu einer Mischung aus Drum 'n' Bass und Synthesizerbeat; in ihren Texten wirbt sie dafür, sich auf eine Sache zu konzentrieren und sich nicht in der Vielfalt des Lebens zu verlaufen.

Mit dem Singen ging es schon früh bei ihr los, erzählt sie. Bevor sie sprechen konnte, summte sie bereits die großen Hits von Michael Jackson mit, die auf dem Plattenspieler ihrer Eltern endlos ihre Runden drehten.

Dass Grace Risch auf Deutsch singt, entwickelte sich erst mit der Zeit. Anfangs hatte sie das Gefühl, die deutsche Sprache würde nicht zu ihrer Musik passen. Also sang sie auf Englisch. Inzwischen findet sie im Deutschen die passenden Worte für ihre Musik. Die Ideen für ihre Lieder kommen ihr in der Straßenbahn, beim Radeln durch Berlin oder auch beim Cappuccinotrinken im „Café Kirsche".

Zu den kleinen Projekten, die sie sonst so ausprobiert, gehört neben dem Modeln seit Kurzem auch das Schauspielern. „Ich hatte überhaupt keine Erfahrungen im Schauspiel, aber es war spannend." Außerdem könnte sie sich aber auch vorstellen, irgendwann mal ein eigenes Café oder Restaurant zu betreiben. „Man muss immer gucken, wo man gerade steht", sagt sie und bestellt sich noch einen Cappuccino. „Im Moment ist mir meine Musik am wichtigsten, aber vielleicht ändert sich das auch noch mal."

Quelle: *Der Tagesspiegel*. 18.11.2014

Lennart Wronkowitz: Modedesigner* mit 16

Er muss weg aus der Provinz, das weiß Lennart Wronkowitz, 16. Er muss seine Heimat verlassen, sonst kann er seinen Traum vergessen. Und sein Traum ist schon ziemlich konkret, Lennart arbeitet bereits daran, ihn zu verwirklichen: Der Gymnasiast aus Soest will als Modedesigner international Karriere machen. „Deshalb muss ich auf lange Sicht auch weg von hier", sagt Lennart, „cool angezogene Leute findet man in Soest nämlich eher nicht." Lennart selbst kleidet sich allerdings überaus ausgefallen. Mit seinen Eigenkreationen fällt der Jung-Designer auf.

Im Alter von 14 Jahren erwachte bei Lennart das Interesse für Design – und er begann, sich Dinge selbst beizubringen: „Ich habe aus Modekatalogen abgezeichnet, und das Nähen habe ich mit Hilfe meiner Mutter, die eine Schneiderlehre gemacht hat, gelernt." Dann gründete er sein eigenes Label und vertreibt seitdem seine Mode im Internet.

Darüber hinaus steht nun die Veröffentlichung seiner dritten Kollektion kurz bevor. Sicher dürfte sein, dass die Stücke der neuen Kollektion alle seine Handschrift tragen: ein gewagter Stil für Menschen, die sich etwas trauen; jugendliche Partymode, die auffällt und alltagstauglich ist.

Für seinen Traum überlegt Lennart, kurz vor dem Abi die Schule zu schmeißen und auf eine Design-Schule zu wechseln. Sein Ziel: den Modeolymp zu erklimmen. „Es wäre schon geil, wenn ich es nach New York schaffen würde", sagt er. Mangelndes Selbstbewusstsein ist eher nicht sein Problem. Und gleichzeitig wirkt Lennart keineswegs abgehoben, sondern bodenständig und erwachsen.

Modedesigner = fashion designer

Quelle: Lattermer, Sabine. ddp/otr. SPIEGEL ONLINE. 26.03.2010

✶ Writing Part 3: Mediation – Young Careers

Your class is taking part in a European project called "Young Careers" and you have to write a text in English about a young German's professional development.
- Read the two articles.
- Choose **one** article.
- Say what the person does and mention at least four **important** aspects of their professional development.
- **Do not translate word for word**, just give the main information.
- Write complete sentences.

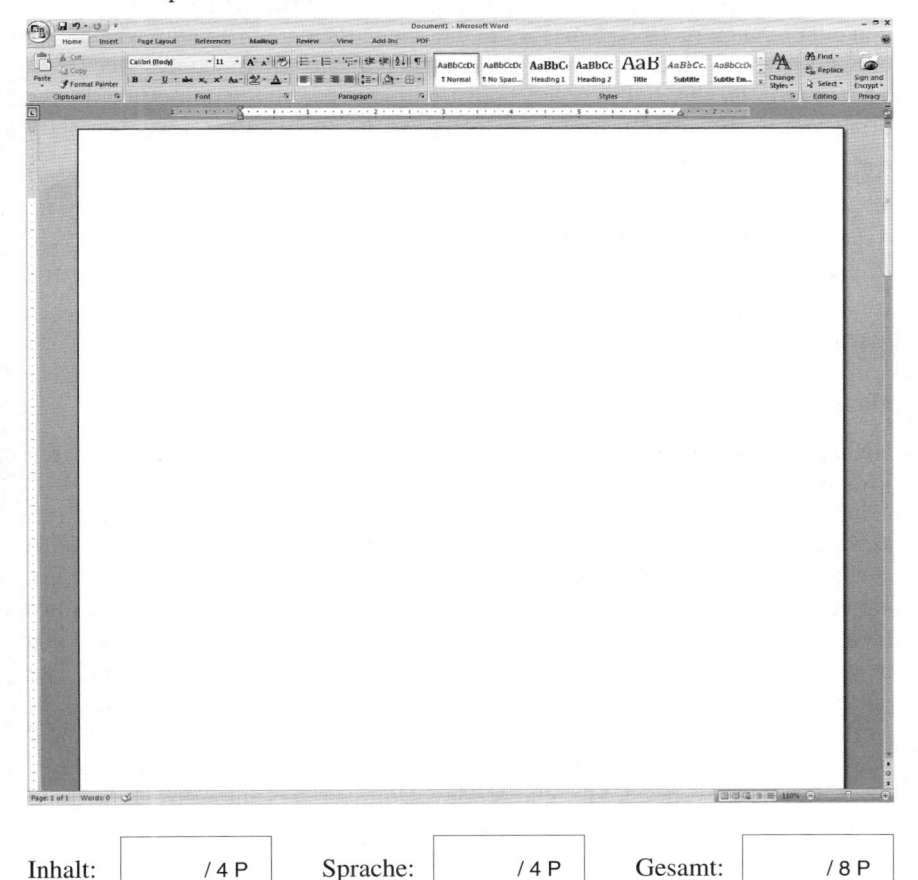

Inhalt: ___ / 4 P   Sprache: ___ / 4 P   Gesamt: ___ / 8 P

Lösungsvorschläge

Listening Part 1: Short Messages

Message One

Hello, this is Orla Devlin speaking. I am the personnel manager of the Metropolitan Hotel in Dublin. This is a message for Jakob Heinemann. You have applied for a job as a cook. We would like to invite you for a job interview next Monday. The interview will be here at our hotel in Parnell Street. By the way, if you arrive by plane, our driver can pick you up from the airport. We can offer you either 9 a.m. or 10.30 a.m. for the interview. Please let us know which time is best for you. You can call between 3 and 5 p.m. any afternoon this week. Just ask for Orla Devlin and the receptionist will connect you to my office. Please bring your health certificate to the interview. It's necessary for kitchen staff. Thank you and goodbye.

1. C

   Hinweis: "You have applied for a job as a cook." (Z. 2/3)

2. B

   Hinweis: "We can offer you either 9 a.m. or 10.30 a.m. for the interview." (Z. 5/6)

Message Two

Hello and welcome to the Natural History Museum. To make your visit more enjoyable please note the following:
Your bags and other personal items will be inspected. Sharp objects such as knives, forks or scissors will be taken from you. Coats and bags can be left in the cloakrooms in the Central Hall next to the café. In the café you can enjoy a great variety of tasty sandwiches, salads and cakes. If you prefer to bring your own food, please visit the Picnic Area on the ground floor for seating and tables. You may take photographs and record videos for personal use in the museum. Our museum collections cover many kinds of animals and plants from all around the world. How about celebrating summer with beautiful butterflies in our popular outdoor Butterfly House? Please note that the Dinosaurs Gallery will be closed for maintenance work until the end of May. Dinosaur toys and souvenirs are still available in our museum's shop next to the main entrance. Enjoy your stay.

3. D

   Hinweis: "Sharp objects such as knives, forks or scissors will be taken from you." (Z. 3/4)

4. B
Hinweis: "Please note that the Dinosaurs Gallery will be closed for maintenance work until the end of May." (Z. 11/12)

Listening Part 2: Radio Ads

Ad 1: Walk

(sounds of footsteps, birds chirping …)
FEMALE: Take a moment, and see if you can guess what I'm doing … I'm getting healthy by walking. Walking daily has tons of health benefits: managing weight, lowering cholesterol and blood pressure, and improving your overall mood. So, whether it's around your neighborhood *(sound of horn honking)* or over your lunch break, just take a walk.
For your free booklet, visit wrinstitute.org or call toll-free 877-957-7575, and find us on facebook and twitter. The Will Rogers Institute – since 1936.

© Will Rogers Institute

5. D
Hinweis: "I'm getting healthy by walking. Walking daily has tons of health benefits …" (Z. 1/2)

Ad 2: Discover the Forest – Busy Family

MOM: So, Jaclyn.
GIRL: Yes Mom …
MOM: I wanted to talk to you about *(BUZZ)* something and … oh wait *(BUZZ)* hold on I just got a text. Oh, there's another one! Wow, busy, busy me! So anyway …
GIRL: *(DING)* Oh wait, Mom, I just got a message *(DING)*. My friends keep commenting on my comment *(DING)*. Oh there's another one! Soooo many comments on my comment!
DAD: Oh I can't wait to watch TV tonight. Playoffffffffffs! *(TV SOUNDS)*
BOY: Hey guys, check out my new video game! Broom boop booom *(VIDEO GAME SOUNDS)*
(All sounds now overlapping, then simultaneously)
GIRL: Wait mom what?
DAD: What hold on …
BOY: Wait a sec, what?
ANNOUNCER: This weekend … *(suddenly, all sounds stop)* Un … plug.
(MUSIC UP) Take your family to the forest. *(FOREST NOISES)* There's nothing in the world like experiencing nature first hand. Trees, paths, blue

20 birds, streams. Getting closer to nature can get you closer to your family. To find the forest nearest you, go to discovertheforest.org. Brought to you by the US Forest Service and the Ad Council.

PSA *"Discover the Forest – Busy Family"* © *2011 The Advertising Council*

6. F
    Hinweis: "Un ... plug. ... Take your family to the forest." (Z. 16/17)

Ad 3: Dating Library

1   MALE: Hey, Rob. Where were you the other day?
    ROB: I was at the library.
    FEMALE: That's hot.
    MALE: No, really, where were you?
5   ROB: I just told you – the Barrie Public Library.
    MALE: Why?
    ROB: Girls like guys who can read. It's ... intelligent and stuff.
    FEMALE: You're so dreamy.
    MALE: Really?
10 ROB: Yeah, watch this ... Hey, Tina! A rose by any other name would smell as sweet.
    FEMALE (II): That's sooo romantic.
    ROB: Ha, ha, yeah!
    FEMALE (III): This dating tip brought to you by the Teen Advisory Board of the
15 Barrie Public Library – enriching your community and social life.

© *Barrie Public Library*

* 7. A
    Hinweis: "Girls like guys who can read." (Z. 7); "This dating tip brought to you by the Teen Advisory Board of the Barrie Public Library – enriching your community and social life." (Z. 14/15)

Ad 4: Burglary

1   FEMALE: There are lots of precautions you can take to stop a burglar breaking in. Listen to the following until you feel reassured. He looks to see if anyone's home. If you always leave a light on, you can stop listening now. He walks up the path. If you have installed a security light, you can stop listening now.
5   He stands by your front door. If you always lock it, you can stop listening now. Without these precautions, a burglar can now enter your home. If you're still listening, maybe it's time to start acting. Most burglaries are pre-

ventable. For more information on how to secure your home, go to metbumblebee.org. Here for London. The Metropolitan Police Service.

http://content.met.police.uk/Campaign/bumblebeecampaign2012. Metropolitan Police Service

8. C

Hinweis: "There are lots of precautions you can take to stop a burglar breaking in." (Z. 1); "Without these precautions, a burglar can now enter your home." (Z. 6)

Listening Part 3: Schools Around the World

(Class Afloat)

Can you imagine living only 15 meters away from your classroom, right next to your classmates and your teachers for 10 months? No? Then you will probably miss the experience of a lifetime. *Class Afloat* is a sailing classroom for students between 16 and 17 years of age. Over the course of a school year your ship will sail to four continents and visit 20 different ports around the world. This is your chance to see other landscapes and learn about other cultures not from books but by really visiting them. Students taking part love things like diving in the Caribbean, visiting temples in Greece and Turkey and climbing sand dunes in the Sahara. These activities are part of everyday life on board. But it's not just fun and games. There are also unpleasant tasks like cleaning the deck or going on night watch. And don't forget the extreme weather conditions at sea – high winds and huge waves. Many students have problems with that. Still, one year aboard *Class Afloat* is an unforgettable experience for everybody.

Based on: http://www.classafloat.com/section/about-class-afloat/about-class-afloat, 26. 03. 2014

(Summerhill School)

"If you don't want to go to classes, you don't have to." This is not what your friends tell you at Summerhill School but what the teachers say. Summerhill School in the East of England is home to about 80 students aged 5 to 18, who live on the school grounds during the school term. This school is popular because it offers almost total freedom. Students and teachers have the same rights and make their school rules together. There is only one rule everybody has to follow: Do what you like as long as you don't harm anyone else. You might think this school will never work if students don't <u>have</u> to do anything. The secret is: Students get bored if they stay away from classes for too long. So pretty soon they realize that going to classes can be fun. This sounds great but of course, there are also negative aspects. One that is often pointed out is that teachers don't plan lessons carefully. But this is something the students accept for the freedom they have.

Based on: http://en.wikipedia.org/wiki/Summerhill_School, 26. 03. 2014

(Padamu Education Centre)

In Europe pupils often see school as a necessary evil. But there are countries in which having the chance to go to school is the only way to escape extreme poverty. One of these schools is The Padamu Residential Education Centre School in a distant mountain region in Bangladesh. About seventy students aged 6–10 live and learn in this boarding school. They come from the villages around the school, but also from far-away places because it's the only school far and wide. Most of these students enjoy going to school simply because they can learn there. But that's not the only thing they love about Padamu. A lot of students are glad to get a free meal every day, others are grateful for free school materials and books. Even if this sounds very good, some students, especially the younger ones, get homesick because they don't often see their parents. But they know – it's only for their own good.

Based on: http://www.takepart.com/article/2011/04/18/jungles-bangladesh-halls-harvard, 26. 03. 2014

9. 16/17 (years) (Z. 4)

* 10. diving (in the Caribbean) (Z. 7/8)/visiting temples (Z. 8)/climbing sand dunes (Z. 8)/seeing other landscapes (Z. 6)/learning about other cultures (Z. 6)/visiting other countries/continents (Z. 4–7)

11. cleaning the deck (Z. 10)/(going on) night watch (Z. 10/11)/bad weather conditions (Z. 11)/(high) winds (Z. 11)/(huge) waves (Z. 12)

12. (East of) England (Z. 3)

13. going to classes (Z. 10)/(total) freedom (Z. 5)/same rights (Z. 5)/make rules together (Z. 6)

* 14. teachers don't plan (lessons/carefully) (Z. 11/12)

15. Bangladesh (Z. 4)

16. (they) can learn there (Z. 7/8)/free meal(s) (Z. 9)/free (school) materials (Z. 9)/free books (Z. 9/10)

17. (some students/younger ones) (get) homesick (Z. 10/11)/don't often see parents (Z. 11)

Listening Part 4: Hotel Mom and Dad

HOST: Good morning and welcome to *Focus on the Family,* a daily discussion about family-related topics with me, your host, Sally Jessy Raphael. Today we'll be talking about grown children who are still living at their parents' homes. Most young adults want to leave home as soon as they can. But for some, that seems to be a difficult move to make.

With me here are Sam Maynard, a 24-year-old college student at the University of San Diego, …

SAM: Hi, there.

HOST: … his mom, Maria Maynard, owner of the Cucina Urbana restaurant, …

MARIA: Good morning.

HOST: … and financial advisor Andrew Chan who has a blog for parents.

CHAN: Thanks for having me.

HOST: Home, sweet home – of all the places in the world, there's no place like home. Maria, what role does the home play in your family's life?

MARIA: My parents were from Italy, and my father was a real mama's boy. He continued to enjoy the luxuries of "Hotel Mama" until he was about 32. What, with his *Mamma* feeding him all that delicious Italian pasta, who could blame him? But this is America. As my children were growing up, I liked to warn them, half jokingly, "Checkout time at this hotel is age 18," I would tell them.

SAM: Yeah, I remember you telling us, but it hasn't worked out that way. You see, a year ago, I asked Mom if I could move back home – with my girlfriend in tow. We wanted to save money when attending college.

MARIA: My husband and I agreed, and Sam and his girlfriend moved into his old bedroom, which is like an apartment of its own with a bathroom, a TV, Internet, and a small fridge. I mean, do you know what the cost of living is in San Diego? It's getting more and more expensive to live in such a big city.

CHAN: If I may step in here … The Maynards are hardly alone. This phenomenon we are talking about here is actually called the "boomerang generation". Millions of young adults in the US and Canada are moving back in with their parents while in college or even after finishing.

HOST: No wonder your parenting blog is so popular! And is the rising cost of living the main reason why adult-age kids are living at home?

CHAN: There are many factors that come into play: a weak economy, a long recession, or not enough jobs – just to name a few. As you know, the job market is very competitive, and with little job security, young adults don't have much financial room to leave home early. This means that many grown children are financially dependent on their parents, and don't learn how to manage their money.

SAM: *(clearing his throat)* Excuse me for interrupting, but when I told my parents that I needed to move back home, we sat down to talk things over. They told me what they expected me to do around the house, which was fine by me. And I've held up my end of the deal, haven't I, Mom?

MARIA: Yes, honey, you have. But on top of room and board, your Dad and I have had to help with extra expenses like your car insurance and cell phone payments. I mean, we want to support you while you're working toward your college degree, but if we're constantly being asked for $20 here and $50 there, it adds up.

HOST: Any suggestions, Mr. Chan?

CHAN: The best way for parents to handle expenses outside of room and board is a weekly or monthly sum. That teaches young adults how to manage their own money and sets a strict limit for how much they will be able to spend. Parents should be firm with their kids from the start and avoid the temptation to give extra financial help, like loans. Something I advise parents on my blog to do is to write up a contract and sign it, so that everything is in black and white and clear to everybody.

MARIA: Hmmm ... A contract would make it more of a serious thing ... Then, Sam, you couldn't say, "We never agreed to that".

SAM: Alright, Mom, let's not get carried away here. I mean, we'd never take advantage of you. And besides, you and Dad seem to have enough money.

CHAN: Are you sure about that, Sam? Having a grown child at home can cost between 8,000 and 18,000 dollars a year. Parents are finding themselves stuck caring for children, sometimes for much longer than they planned – often damaging their own financial health and using money they have saved up for their old age.

MARIA: It's true. Since Sam moved back home, my husband and I have delayed a life-long dream of ours – to go on a cruise in the Caribbean, and my husband, who is now 60, has to keep working full-time, although he was planning to reduce his working hours.

SAM: Oh, Mom, I didn't realize. But we are happy with these living arrangements, right? The house is so close to my college campus, and it's not like I plan on staying until I'm 30 or 35 or even until I'm married like Grandpa *Nonno* did. You'd never actually kick me out of the house, would you?

MARIA: Well, we never did set a limit for how long you are allowed to stay, but you've been back for a year now and seem to have gotten quite comfortable at home ... I mean, your father and I have given up a lot of privacy because you are living with us again. We would like to have our nest back for ourselves someday, you know.

CHAN: If you don't mind me saying so, Mrs. Maynard, the biggest mistake parents make is not to say from the start when they expect their child to move out. As a rule of thumb, parents shouldn't allow their kids to live with them longer than, say, a year and a half. The longer children stay, the harder it is for them to leave.

HOST: And the more expensive it gets.

CHAN: Exactly. One approach to encourage kids to move out is for parents to give their child a sum of money every month that will slowly be reduced over time. It's a strategy I am using with my own 20-year-old daughter who is still living at home. As my wife and I reduce her allowance by about $50 a month, she is taking on more responsibility.

HOST: Isn't taking on more and more responsibility what growing up is all about? Let's hold on to that thought. We'll go into more detail right after this commercial break, *(fade out)* brought to you by your local …

Based on: http://online.wsj.com/articles/SB10001424127887323699704578326583020869940, 22. 01. 2016;
http://www.spiegel.de/international/europe/bad-economy-means-young-europeans-having-trouble-leaving-home-a-877616.html, 22. 01. 2016;
http://www.canada.com/story.html?id=83904bd8-3118-45c8-bc4c-cabd2a8ef8db, 22. 01. 2016

18. B
Hinweis: " 'Checkout time at this hotel is age 18' " *(Z. 19)*

19. C
Hinweis: "We wanted to save money when attending college." *(Z. 23)*

20. B
Hinweis: "This means that many grown children are financially dependent on their parents, and don't learn how to manage their money." *(Z. 38–40)*

* 21. A
Hinweis: "… your Dad and I have had to help with extra expenses like your car insurance and cell phone payments." *(Z. 45–47)*

* 22. B
Hinweis: "Parents should be firm with their kids from the start and avoid the temptation to give extra financial help, like loans. Something I advise parents on my blog to do is to write up a contract and sign it, so that everything is in black and white and clear to everybody." *(Z. 54–57)*

* 23. C
Hinweis: "Having a grown child at home can cost between 8,000 and 18,000 dollars a year. Parents are finding themselves stuck caring for children … often damaging their own financial health and using money they have saved up for their old age." *(Z. 62–66)*

* 24. B
Hinweis: "… your father and I have given up a lot of privacy because you are living with us again. We would like to have our nest back for ourselves someday …" *(Z. 77–79)*

* 25. B
  Hinweis: "This means that many grown children are financially dependent on their parents, and don't learn how to manage their money." (Z. 38–40); "The longer children stay, the harder it is for them to leave." (Z. 83/84)

Reading Part 1: Apps

1./2. C, E
  Hinweis: "What he needs is a cool running app …"; "… one that helps him remember to do his homework."
  → app C: "With this app you will run like never before."
  → app E: "The app also lets you set reminders so you never forget what assignments and reading you need to complete."

3./4. B, D
  Hinweis: "… trains the youth team of her soccer club. They are good but they don't score."; "… she loves to go to concerts with her friends. If an app could only tell her beforehand where they all plan to go."
  → app B: "… improve soccer skills …"
  → app D: "… see which events your friends are going to!"

5./6. D, F
  Hinweis: "… a festival addict who always wants to be the first to get the tickets. If there is an app she needs, it is one that makes buying and selling tickets as easy as pie."; "… an app that can notify her closest friends or family if necessary."
  → app D: "Get tickets and quickly access all of your tickets and event information from your phone."; "… and sell tickets to any event imaginable …"
  → app F: "… for those situations when you need to quickly and discreetly get help from your friends or family."

7./8. A, F
  Hinweis: "Instead of staring out of the window he would like to listen to news stories or blogs …"; "… he has already experienced some dangerous situations on the train. Some friends could easily help him out if he could contact them somehow."
  → app A: "Whether commuting … let this app accompany you and enrich your day. This app is perfect for you if you like podcasts, listen to audio books or prefer to consume other audio content on the go."
  → app F: "… for those situations when you need to quickly and discreetly get help from your friends or family."

9./10. A, G
Hinweis: "She needs to work on her English a little. An app that explains music clips or talk shows would be great for her. Listening to some authentic speakers who read the news in an app would be a perfect exercise, too."

→ app A: "Listen to an ever growing catalogue of articles from the world's best publishers and bloggers narrated by professional voice-actors. ... This app is perfect for you if you like podcasts, listen to audio books ..."

→ app G: "You'll learn English as it's spoken in real life. Browse through the huge database of the app and find the latest music videos, popular talk shows, news, inspiring talks and funny commercials. This app makes it really easy to watch English videos."

Reading Part 2: Short Texts

* 11. D
Hinweis: "Next time you check my ticket we should swap numbers."

12. C
Hinweis: "The smartest card in my wallet? It's a library card."

13. B
Hinweis: "... many fire deaths are caused by people attempting to cook or smoke while under the influence of alcohol."; "Don't put yourself – or your family – at risk to fire."

14. A
Hinweis: "Exercise is Medicine."

15. A
Hinweis: "The Dinosaurs gallery is closed from 8 to 19 September for a big summer clean."

16. C
Hinweis: "... we will collect your rubbish and recycling on the days below."

Reading Part 3: Distracted Walking

17. C
Hinweis: "Suddenly he stumbles, loses his balance and falls over the side, landing head first on the tracks." (Z. 2/3)

* 18. B
    * *Hinweis:* "*distracted walking ... walking while talking on a phone, texting with his head down, listening to music, or playing a video game.*" (Z. 7–10)
* 19. A
    * *Hinweis:* "*... placing signs on crosswalks and sidewalks at busy intersections urging pedestrians to 'Look up ...'*" (Z. 15/16)
* 20. D
    * *Hinweis:* "*an April Fool's Day joke*" (Z. 17); "*'... once they realized we were going to take the e-lane away, got mad because they thought it was really helpful to not have people get in their way while they were walking and texting ...'*" (Z. 20–22)
* 21. C
    * *Hinweis:* "*... a regulation forbidding pedestrians from using cellphones, headphones or other distracting electronic devices while crossing the tracks of its rail system on the streets of Salt Lake City.*" (Z. 23–25)
* 22. C
    * *Hinweis:* "*... tumbled into a large fountain directly in front of her and got soaking wet.*" (Z. 35/36)
* 23. B
    * *Hinweis:* "*... pedestrians often think they're in control and that it's all the other fools on their phones who aren't watching what they're doing.*" (Z. 42/43); "*'People think they can do it, that they are somehow better.'*" (Z. 47)
* 24. A
    * *Hinweis:* "*The group that talked on the cellphone walked slightly slower and went off course a bit more than before, but the texting group walked slower, went off course 61 percent more and overshot the target 13 percent more.*" (Z. 55–58)
* 25. A
    * *Hinweis:* Der Text befasst sich ganz allgemein mit dem Phänomen des "distracted walking". Überschrift C mit ihrem Fokus auf "distracted driving" scheidet daher aus. Auch Überschrift D kommt nicht infrage, da die ständige Benutzung von Smartphones insgesamt kritisch gesehen wird. Dennoch scheidet auch Überschrift B aus, weil Verbote nur als Extremlösung gesehen werden ("*'I mean, it's our phone. We should be able to use it and walk and talk if we choose to ...'*"; Z. 27/28). Es bleibt also Lösung A, die in ihrer allgemeinen Warnung vor den Gefahren der Ablenkung durch technische Geräte auch am besten passt.

Writing Part 1: Rent a Bed

Beispiellösung:
Age: 16
City/Town: Berlin, Germany
1. (on the) sofa in my room
2. (my) family and (my) dog
3. no smoking, be home by midnight
4. park (nearby), (quiet) neighbourhood
5. toothbrush, shampoo, good sense of humour

Writing Part 2: Trip to Berlin

✎ Hinweis: Lies dir die Nachricht des Bloggers gut durch, damit du in deiner Antwort auf alle seine Fragen eingehen kannst. Er fragt nach der Größe von Berlin und nach einer Gegend, die du für seinen Aufenthalt empfehlen würdest. Außerdem möchte er etwas über dein Stadtviertel erfahren: Welche Vor- und Nachteile hat das Leben dort deiner Meinung nach? Abschließend sollst du noch die Frage beantworten, ob du gerne in Deutschland lebst.

Beispiellösung:
Hi City Hopper,

It's a great idea that you want to come to Berlin. It is a very nice city and really big with about 3.5 million people. I would stay in Mitte, which is also the area where I live. It has become a very popular neighbourhood and it has a lot of cafés, bars, shops and two flea markets on Sunday, which I like. It is close to many forms of public transportation and there are also a couple of parks nearby. What I dislike though, is that it has become so trendy that the rents have doubled, and it is virtually impossible to find an affordable flat in the area. When I hear about the situation in other parts of the world, however, I'm glad that I live in Germany. It is very organised, safe, and doesn't seem corrupt compared to many other countries.

Best regards,
City Dweller

(151 words)

✶ Writing Part 3: Mediation – Young Careers

*✎ **Hinweis:** Du kannst hier aus zwei verschiedenen Texten wählen. Es empfiehlt sich, den Text auszuwählen, über den du leichter auf Englisch schreiben kannst. Wichtige Punkte, die du auf jeden Fall erwähnen solltest, sind der Beruf der von dir gewählten Person und mindestens vier Stationen ihres beruflichen Werdegangs.*

Beispiellösung zu Grace Risch:
Grace Risch: Singer from Berlin
Grace Risch is a 32-year-old singer from Berlin with Nigerian roots whose first single is "Kleine Welt" ("Small world"). Her music is a mixture of Drum 'n' Bass and synthesizer beats. She started singing even before she could speak and her first idol was Michael Jackson. At first, she wrote her songs in English but these days sings in German because it is now easy for her to find the right words for her music. She also does some acting and modelling and can imagine running a café or restaurant one day. (92 words)

Beispiellösung zu Lennart Wronkowitz:
Lennart Wronkowitz: Fashion designer at 16
Lennart Wronkowitz is 16 years old and already a fashion designer. He is trying to make an international career, and that is why he will have to leave the small town he comes from. He has been interested in fashion design since he was 14 and learned to sew from his mother, who is a tailor. He founded his own label and sells his clothes online. Meanwhile, he is about to show his third collection, which is trendy and designed for young people who want to stand out in a crowd. He might transfer to a design school before finishing his A-levels in order to achieve his dream of moving to New York someday. (114 words)

Bildnachweis:
S. 2016-1: Hotelrezeption © shock/fotolia.com; Chauffeur © Konstantin Sutyagin/fotolia.com; Koch © fotoinfot/fotolia.com; Büroangestellter © contrastwerkstatt/fotolia.com; S. 2016-2: Sandwich © Nayashkova Olga. Shutterstock; Rucksack © Tereshchenko Dmitry. Shutterstock; Videokamera © Fabio Alcini. Shutterstock; Besteck © Ethan boisvert. Shutterstock; Museumsshop © Sainaniritu/Dreamstime.com; Dinosaurier-Ausstellung © TOSHIFUMI KITAMURA/AFP/Getty Images; S. 2016-3: Schmetterling Hand © Can Stock Photo Inc./nikkytok; Museumscafé © Wavebreak Premium. Shutterstock; Stereoanlage © PRILL Mediendesign/fotolia.de; S. 2016-4: Class Afloat © Class Afloat, Lunenburg, Nova Scotia; Summerhill School © Summerhill School, Leiston, Suffolk; indische Schulklasse © Samrat35/Dreamstime.com; S. 2016-8: "Jamal" © Image Source; "Afifa" © Jules Selmes. Pearson Education Ltd; "Grace" © Samuel Borges Photography. Shutterstock; S. 2016-9: "Ryan" © Jules Selmes. Pearson Education Ltd; "Charlotte" © Tudor Photography. Pearson Education Ltd; S. 2016-10: Coach's eye © TechSmith; S. 2016-12: Luol Deng Library Card © American Library Association; S. 2016-13: Dangerous Mix © Fire Marshals Public Fire Safety Council; Exercise is Medicine © American College of Sports Medicine, Inc. (ACSM); S. 2016-14: Rubbish collection © http://beebokay.blogspot.de/; S. 2016-15: Frau mit Smartphone © nenetus/fotolia.com; S. 2016-22: Grace Risch © imago/VIADATA; Lennart Wronkowitz © ddp images/dapd

Notizen

Notizen

Jetzt mal **BUTTER** bei die Fische.

Liebe Kundin, lieber Kunde,

der STARK Verlag hat das Ziel, Sie effektiv beim Lernen zu unterstützen. In welchem Maße uns dies gelingt, wissen Sie am besten. Deshalb bitten wir Sie, uns Ihre Meinung zu den STARK-Produkten in dieser Umfrage mitzuteilen:

www.stark-verlag.de/feedback

Als Dankeschön verlosen wir einmal jährlich, zum 31. Juli, unter allen Teilnehmern ein aktuelles Samsung-Tablet. Für nähere Informationen und die Teilnahmebedingungen folgen Sie dem Internetlink.

Herzlichen Dank!

Haben Sie weitere Fragen an uns?
Sie erreichen uns telefonisch **0180 3 179000***
per E-Mail **info@stark-verlag.de**
oder im Internet unter **www.stark-verlag.de**

Lernen ▪ Wissen ▪ Zukunft
STARK

*9 Cent pro Min. aus dem deutschen Festnetz, Mobilfunk bis 42 Cent pro Min. Aus dem Mobilfunknetz wählen Sie die Festnetznummer: **08167 9573-0**

Erfolgreich durch die Abschlussprüfung mit den **STARK** Reihen

Abschlussprüfung

Anhand von Original-Aufgaben die Prüfungssituation trainieren. Schülergerechte Lösungen helfen bei der Leistungskontrolle.

Training

Prüfungsrelevantes Wissen schülergerecht präsentiert. Übungsaufgaben mit Lösungen sichern den Lernerfolg.

Klassenarbeiten

Praxisnahe Übungen für eine gezielte Vorbereitung auf Klassenarbeiten.

STARK in Klassenarbeiten

Schülergerechtes Training wichtiger Themenbereiche für mehr Lernerfolg und bessere Noten.

Kompakt-Wissen

Kompakte Darstellung des prüfungsrelevanten Wissens zum schnellen Nachschlagen und Wiederholen.

Und vieles mehr auf www.stark-verlag.de

Den Abschluss in der Tasche – und dann?

In den **STARK** Ratgebern findest du alle Informationen für einen erfolgreichen Start in die berufliche Zukunft.

Sandra Gehde
Ausbildungsplatzsuche für Durchstarter
Erfolg bei Stellensuche, Bewerbung und Vorstellungsgespräch

Hesse/Schrader
Die perfekte Bewerbungsmappe für Ausbildungsplatzsuchende
Mit den besten Beispielen erfolgreicher Kandidaten

Hesse/Schrader
Testtraining 2000plus
Einstellungs- und Eignungstests erfolgreich bestehen

Angela Verse-Herrmann
Dieter Herrmann
Joachim Edler
Der große Berufswahltest
So entscheide ich mich richtig

Hesse/Schrader
Testtraining Polizei und Feuerwehr
Einstellungs- und Eignungstests erfolgreich bestehen
Schutz- und Kriminalpolizei, Bundespolizei, Bundeswehr, Verfassungsschutz und Feuerwehr

Alle Titel zu Beruf & Karriere
www.berufundkarriere.de

Bestellungen bitte direkt an
STARK Verlagsgesellschaft mbH & Co. KG · Postfach 1852 · 85318 Freising
Tel. 0180 3 179000* · Fax 0180 3 179001* · www.stark-verlag.de · info@stark-verlag.de

Lernen • Wissen • Zukunft
STARK

*9 Cent pro Min. aus dem deutschen Festnetz, Mobilfunk bis 42 Cent pro Min. Aus dem Mobilfunknetz wählen Sie die Festnetznummer: **08167 9573-0**